A RUMOR
OF ANGELS

Peter L. Berger is University Professor and Director of the Institute for the Study of Economic Culture at Boston University. His publications in the field of religion include *The Heretical Imperative: Contemporary Possibilities of Religious Affirmation*, as well as *The Noise of Solemn Assemblies* and *The Precarious Vision*, both critical analyses of Protestant life and thought in America. His other works include the well-known *Invitation to Sociology*, *The Social Construction of Reality*, and *The Sacred Canopy*.

PETER L. BERGER

A RUMOR
OF ANGELS

MODERN SOCIETY
AND THE REDISCOVERY
OF THE SUPERNATURAL

EXPANDED WITH
A NEW INTRODUCTION
BY THE AUTHOR

ANCHOR BOOKS
DOUBLEDAY
New York London Toronto
Sydney Auckland

AN ANCHOR BOOK

PUBLISHED BY DOUBLEDAY

a division of Bantam Doubleday Dell Publishing Group, Inc.
666 Fifth Avenue, New York, New York 10103

ANCHOR BOOKS, DOUBLEDAY, and the portrayal of an anchor
are trademarks of Doubleday, a division of Bantam Doubleday
Dell Publishing Group, Inc.

A Rumor of Angels was originally published in hardcover by
Doubleday in 1969. The Anchor Books edition is
published by arrangement with Doubleday.

Book design by Patrice Fodero

LIBRARY OF CONGRESS CATALOGING-IN-PUBLICATION DATA

Berger, Peter L.
    A rumor of angels : modern society and the rediscovery of the
supernatural / Peter L. Berger. — Exp., with a new introd. by the
author.
        p.   cm.
    Includes bibliographical references.
    1. Religion and sociology.   2. Supernatural (Theology)   3. Holy,
The.   4. Experience (Religion)   I. Title.
BL60.B41   1990
200—dc20   90-34900
                                                                 CIP

ISBN 0-385-41592-3

Copyright © 1969, 1990, by Peter L. Berger
ALL RIGHTS RESERVED
PRINTED IN THE UNITED STATES OF AMERICA
ANCHOR BOOKS EDITIONS: 1969, 1990
RRC

To the Memory of
Frederick Neumann
1899–1967

Contents

Contents

Introduction to
the 1990 Edition

It is now over twenty years ago that I wrote *A Rumor of Angels*. What is one to say after all this time? Looking again at things one has written long ago is quite often very much like meeting up with a long-lost lover: Embarrassed, one is at a loss for words; silently, to oneself, one says, "How could I?" It is quite gratifying to me that this particular book does not put me in such a predicament. It does not embarrass me. What is more, there are relatively few passages in it that I would now take back or seriously reformulate. So, the first observation I can make here is, in the old proofreader's terminology, "stet"—"Let it stand!" I would not want to be accused of smugness. There are other writings of mine, some more recent than this one, which do embarrass me greatly, that I would want to revoke or at least to alter substantially. But not *A Rumor of Angels*.

In this book, after repeating a number of propositions I had made in slightly earlier writings about religion in the modern world, I tried to make two points. First, I wanted to show how the intellectual tools of the social sciences, which had contributed greatly to the loss of credibility of religion, could be turned on the very ideas that had thus discredited supernatural views of the world and on the people propagating those ideas. I called this project "relativizing the relativizers." And second, I wanted to draw a very rough sketch of an approach to theologizing that began with ordinary human experience, more specifically with elements of that experience that point toward a reality beyond the ordinary. I called this approach "inductive" and I indicated a number of experiential complexes that could be considered "signals of transcendence." I suggested that here was to be found the basis of a theological program rooted in what Europeans call philosophical anthropology and in the broad tradition of liberal Protestantism stretching back to Friedrich Schleiermacher. Unlike many expressions of the liberal Protestant tradition, however, such a program would not secularize the religious definitions of reality; on the contrary, it would, as it were, transcendentalize secularity. I made it emphatically clear that I was not in a position to supply this theological program beyond the preliminary sketch, thus inviting the reproach that one should put up or shut up (some critics accepted the invitation).

I would reaffirm both these points today. The first I could make today much more amply; the second, alas, I could not elaborate upon very much further even now. I do have an excuse for this discrepancy. In showing how the social-scientific perspective can, as it were, be turned back upon itself, I was simply doing my own professional job. I am, after all, a sociologist, so certified and credentialed. The second point (as I said quite clearly at the time) is a theological one; sociology is barely relevant to it, and I have no credentials as a theologian. Contrary to the Latin adage, *both* life and art are short; mostly, one only gets to practice a single art in a lifetime.

At precisely the time that I was writing *A Rumor of Angels*, through a series of biographical accidents, I became interested in questions of Third World development and modernization. These questions have remained in the center of my work as a sociologist ever since. Many of these questions have little if anything to do with religion; most of them have very direct practical and indeed political relevance. Yet, in a very general way, all of my work in this area has served the project of "relativizing the relativizers." The more conscious one becomes of the immense variety of human thought and action in this world, the more one puts in proportion the peculiar ideas and institutions that we subsume under the heading of "modernity." I am convinced that sociology today must be a cross-national, cross-cultural discipline, not because of some moral purpose of all-embracing understanding and tolerance, but because it is no longer possible to understand one society without understanding it in comparison with others. This kind of sociology, though, becomes in fact an overall critique of modernity. It discloses the naïveté and the parochialism of those Western "cultured despisers of religion" who have been the interlocutors (real or imagined) of so much recent Christian theology. Thus, if I wanted to, I could today describe more fully just how relative (and ipso facto vulnerable to sociological "location") is the worldview of modern secularity. This would be an amplification of the argument in *A Rumor of Angels*; it would not substantially alter it.

The other point, the suggestion of an anthropologically grounded approach to theology, I have in the interval been able to pursue only sporadically. In 1975 I was instrumental, together with Richard Neuhaus, in convening the group that issued the so-called "Hartford Appeal for Theological Affirmation." The core of this statement was an insistence that Christian faith refers to the transcendent and not to this or that secular agenda. It came at a time when very powerful forces in mainline Protestantism and increasingly in the Roman Catholic church were pushing in precisely the opposite direction. After a flurry of attention, much of it negative, the Hartford Appeal was more or less forgotten.

In 1979 another book of mine was published, *The Heretical Imperative*, in which I tried to push the theological agenda proposed in *Rumor* a little further. I would now question whether I succeeded very well in this and the book, perhaps deservedly, did not receive much attention. I did a few things to my own satisfaction if not that of my critics: I explained more fully why I would continue to use the much-maligned term "supernatural"; I placed an "inductive" approach to theology in a larger context of available theological options; and, as the final thrust of the book, I argued that a new impetus for Christian theology might come from its encounter with the great religious traditions of Asia. The last argument was a natural outcome of my sociological globe-trotting; I'm somewhat less persuaded of it now, after ten more years of thus trotting around. In any case, around the same time I was instrumental in bringing together a group of very competent people interested in new ways of engaging in inter-religious dialogue. The early papers produced by the group (which lasted for about two years) were published under the title *The Other Side of God*. Here too, I'm afraid, is a very sketchy, preliminary outline of an intellectual program which I have not been able to realize.

Martin Marty, in reviewing *A Rumor of Angels* upon its original publication, opined that here "may be the first plank in a platform for the 1970s." He could not have been more wrong. Not only the 1970s, but the 1980s as well, saw Christian theologians moving in the diametrically opposite direction in droves. Politics, not transcendence, was declared as the proper concern of Christians and ipso facto of Christian theology. Far from trying to discern the "signals of transcendence" in ordinary human reality, theologians were exposing the signals of secular interests in the traditionally transcendent referents of religion, and the religious traditions were reinterpreted so as to legitimate this or that secular purpose—socialism, feminism, black consciousness, the environment, or what-have-you. I do not as yet see any signs that this wave of secularizing ideas has exhausted itself. On the contrary, many of these ideas have been firmly institutionalized in church bureaucracies and intellectual establishments, to the point where even mild dissent from these political orthodoxies is met with howls of derision and hatred. I would say that despite the outwardly greater calm, the theological scene today is far more dismal than it was twenty years ago. Perhaps the suggestions made in *A Rumor of Angels* will contribute to a theological platform in the 1990s. Given the theological weather map as of now, I'm not holding my breath.

This edition of the book contains a number of essays written after its original publication, all following up one or another theme in *Rumor*. "A Lutheran View of the Elephant," which was originally an address to a gathering of (naturally) Lutheran church people, spins out the proposition that the comic is one of the most fundamental "signals of transcendence" in human experience. "A Funeral in Calcutta" and "From Secularity to World Religions," the first written right after my first visit to India, are both concerned with the encounter between Christian faith and the religions of Asia.

The last two essays reprinted here are quite recent. "Moral Judgment and Political Action" is a polemic against the widespread notion that a sense of moral purity, rather than an assessment of practical consequences, should animate involvement in politics. And the essay on "Religious Liberty" makes once again the point that human life, even in its most secular aspects, is enriched by the windows on transcendence which it is the task of religion to keep open. Put differently, keeping alive the rumor of angels is to contribute to the humanization of our time.

—P.L.B.
Boston, 1990

Preface

This book is concerned with the possibility of theological thinking in our present situation. It asks whether such thinking is possible at all today and, if so, in what way. The first question is answered affirmatively, and the answer is, up to a point, supported by an argument that derives from sociology. In the very tentative approaches made to an answer of the second question, sociology is of little if any use. It should, therefore, be very clear that I can claim no authority as a sociologist for a good deal of what follows here. This means that I'm sticking my neck out in the most blatant way, and I should probably explain my motives.

In a recent book, *The Sacred Canopy—Elements of a Sociological Theory of Religion* (Garden City, N.Y., Doubleday, 1967), I attempted to summarize what seem to me to be certain essential features of a sociological perspective on religion and I tried to apply this perspective to an analysis of the contemporary religious situation. I have been trained in a sociological tradition shaped by Max Weber and so I tried, to the best of my ability, to keep my statements "value-free." The result was a theoretical work that, quite apart from the technical jargon in which it had to be presented, read like a treatise on atheism, at least in parts. The analysis of the contemporary situation with which it ended could easily be read (and, as far as my intentions were concerned, misread) as a counsel of despair for religion in the modern world. For better or for worse, my self-understanding is not exhausted by the fact that I am a sociologist. I also consider myself a Christian, though I have not yet found the heresy into which my theological views would comfortably fit. All this made me uneasy about the possible effect of *The Sacred Canopy* upon the unwary reader and so I added an appendix that dealt with some possible theological implications of the book's argument. This way out did not satisfy me, and the present book is the result of this dissatisfaction.

In what follows I try to say what I have to say as simply as I can and without forcing the reader to go first through the conceptual and terminological apparatus with which I habitually carry on my business as a sociologist. I have found a few technical terms indispensable, but I have tried to keep these to a minimum. This book, then, is not particularly addressed to sociologists and does not presuppose the debatable benefits of a sociological education. It is addressed to anyone with a concern for religious questions and the willingness to think about them systematically. I hope that it may have something to say to theologians, though I'm fully aware of my lack of expertise in theology. In view of the non-technical (I'm tempted to say unprofessional) character of the book, I have also kept the notes to a minimum and almost entirely limited them to references in English. The relatively frequent references to previous writings of my own should in no way be construed as a conviction on my part that these writings are terribly important or as advice to the reader to go back to them. But every process of thinking must be a conversation with oneself and particularly with one's previous thought, and one cannot at each step start all over again from the beginning. Not to have to do this should perhaps be one of the fringe benefits of having written more than one book.

I suppose one sticks one's neck out when it comes to things one deems important. I think that religion is of very great importance at any time and of particular importance in our own time. If theologizing means simply any systematic reflection about religion, then it would seem plausible to regard it as too important to leave to the theological experts. Ergo, one must stick out one's neck. This implies impertinence as well as modesty. To try at all may well be impertinent. This should make it all the clearer that the effort is tentative and the result unfinished.

Some of the ideas that follow were discussed at length with Richard Neuhaus. I would like to express my great appreciation of his interest and suggestions on these occasions.

I have dedicated this book to my first teacher in theology. I know that he would not have liked many of its conclusions, but I venture to hope that he would have approved the basic intention.

—P.L.B.
New York, Fall 1968

A RUMOR
OF ANGELS

1

The Alleged Demise of the Supernatural

If commentators on the contemporary situation of religion agree about anything, it is that the supernatural has departed from the modern world. This departure may be stated in such dramatic formulations as "God is dead" or "the post-Christian era." Or it may be undramatically assumed as a global and probably irreversible trend. Thus the "radical theologian" Thomas Altizer tells us with the solemnity of a confessional pronouncement that "we must realize that the death of God is an historical event, that God has died in our cosmos, in our history, in our *Existenz*."[1] And Herman Kahn and Anthony Wiener, of the Hudson Institute, in their fascinating attempt to project the course of the final third of this century, manage to do so with only minimal mention of religion and on the assumption that twentieth-century cultures will continue to be increasingly "sensate"—a term coined by the late Harvard sociologist Pitirim Sorokin, and defined by Kahn and Wiener as "empirical, this-worldly, secular, humanistic, pragmatic, utilitarian, contractual, epicurean or hedonistic, and the like."[2]

1

The departure of the supernatural has been received in a variety of moods—with prophetic anger, in deep sorrow, with gleeful triumph, or simply as an emotionally unprovocative fact. But the spokesman of traditional religion who thunders against a godless age, the "progressive" intellectual who hails its coming, and the dispassionate analyst who merely registers it have in common the recognition that such, indeed, is our situation—an age in which the divine, at least in its classical forms, has receded into the background of human concern and consciousness.

The term "supernatural" has been justly criticized on a number of grounds. Historians of religion and cultural anthropologists have pointed out that the term suggests the division of reality into a closed system of rationally comprehensible "nature" and a mysterious world somehow beyond it, a peculiarly modern conception, which is misleading if one seeks to understand the religious notions of primitive or archaic cultures. Biblical scholars have criticized the term as failing to convey the concreteness and historical character of the Israelite religious experience, and Christian theologians attacked it as offending the world-affirming implications of the doctrine of the incarnation, if not indeed of the doctrine of creation. Nevertheless the term, particularly in its everyday usage, denotes a fundamental category of religion, namely the assertion or belief that there is *an other reality*, and one of ultimate significance for man, which transcends the reality within which our everyday experience unfolds. It is this fundamental assumption about reality, rather than this or that historical variation of it, that is allegedly defunct or in the process of becoming defunct in the modern world.

The historian of religion, Rudolf Otto, in *The Idea of the Holy* (originally published in German in 1917) attempted what may still be regarded as a definitive description of this "otherness" of religious experience. Otto emphasized that the sacred (that is, the reality man believes he encounters in religious experience) is "totally other" than ordinary, human phenomena, and in this "otherness" the sacred impresses man as an overwhelming, awesome, and strangely fascinating power.

As one might expect, there has been extensive controversy since then as to the validity of Otto's delineation of the sacred as the religious category par excellence in all cultures. Once more, however, these scholarly debates may be left aside. Instead, let us look at the ordinary world, which some philosophers have called the *Lebenswelt*, or "life-world," within which we carry on our "normal" activities in collaboration with other men. This is the arena of most of our projects in life, whose reality is strongest and thus the most "natural" in our consciousness. This, in the words of the social philosopher Alfred Schutz, is "the world of daily life which the wide-awake, grown-up man who acts in it and upon it amidst his fellow-man experiences within the natural attitude as a reality."[3] It is to this domain of taken-for-granted, "natural" experience (*not* necessarily to "nature" in the sense of, say, the eighteenth-century rationalists) that religion posits a "supernatural" reality.

As cultural anthropologists have pointed out, the everyday life of primitive man was, like ours, dominated by empirical, pragmatic, utilitarian imperatives geared to "this world"; he could hardly have solved the basic problems of survival if it had not been. This was even more true of daily life in the great ancient civilizations. The preoccupation with "natural" consciousness is not at all peculiar to the modern age. Someone once remarked that most present-day Anglo-American philosophers have the same conception of reality as that held by a slightly drowsy, middle-aged businessman right after lunch. Very probably slightly drowsy, middle-aged tribal warriors and ancient Greeks held very similar conceptions right after *their* lunches. But primitive and ancient men also accepted the idea of another, supernatural world of divine beings and forces as a background to the ordinary world and assumed that "the other world" impinged on this one in a variety of ways. This suggests that at least part of the reason why we today have embraced what we consider the "rationality" (or "naturalism") of modern science and philosophy is because we wish to maintain that "natural" consciousness is the only possible or desirable one—a point that will be taken up again later.

There is a German fairy tale about a young apprentice who is disturbed by the fact that he has never been able to experience gruesomeness and deliberately subjects himself to all sorts of situations that are reputed to evoke such feelings. The spiritual adventure of modern man seems to have been motivated by the opposite aim of *un*learning any conceivable metaphysical terror. If the idea about the demise of the supernatural is correct, then the unlearning effort has indeed succeeded. How much evidence is there in support of the idea?

The answer hinges on what might be called the secularization theory of modern culture—using the word secularization not in the sense of what has happened with social institutions (such as, for example, the separation of church and state), but as applying to processes inside the human mind, that is, a secularization of *consciousness*. Here the empirical evidence is not very satisfactory. Considering the importance of the question, one might have expected professional observers of the contemporary scene, especially sociologists, to invest some energy in an attempt to provide answers. But in recent years sociologists, with very few exceptions, have shown very little interest, probably because they have sworn allegiance to a scientific "progressivism" that regards religion as a vanishing leftover from the dark ages of superstition and do not care to invest their energies in the study of a moribund phenomenon. The fairly small group of sociologists who have taken the sociology of religion as their professional specialty have not been terribly helpful either.[4] They have not looked on religion as moribund, if only for reasons of professional self-respect, but they have regarded it almost exclusively in terms of the traditional religious institutions—that is, most recent sociology of religion

4

has been a sociology *of the churches*. And it is from this somewhat restricted perspective that a good deal of sound evidence has, indeed, been accumulated on secularization. The largest body of data, most of which refer to Europe, comes from the school of so-called "religious sociology," which is largely Catholic-inspired.[5] Recently there have been some interesting attempts quite distinct from this school to uncover motives for religious participation in America with the use of more sophisticated research tools.[6]

On the basis of this evidence one can say with some confidence that *churchly* religiosity (that is, religious belief and practice within the traditions of the principal Christian churches) has been on the decline in modern society. In Europe this has generally taken the form of a progressive decline in institutional participation (attendance at worship, use of the sacraments, and the like), though there are important class differences in this. In America, on the contrary, there has been an increase in participation (as measured by church membership figures), though there are good reasons to think that the motives for participation have changed greatly from the traditional ones. It is safe to say that, compared to earlier historical periods, fewer Americans today adhere to the churches out of a burning desire for salvation from sin and hellfire, while many do so out of a desire to provide moral instruction for their children and direction for their family life, or just because it is part of the life style of their particular neighborhood. The difference between the European and American patterns has been aptly characterized by the sociologist Thomas Luckmann as, respectively, "secularization from without" and "secularization from within." In both cases there is strong evidence that traditional religious beliefs have become empty of meaning not only in large sections of the general population but even among many people who, with whatever motives, continue to belong to a church. All this, of course, leaves open the question of whether there may not be genuinely religious forces outside the traditional Christian or churchly frame of reference. Also, since sociologists and their ilk have been around for only a rather short time, it is not clear to what extent their findings can be rigorously compared with the situation in previous periods, for which different and only imperfectly comparable data are available. Sociologists, equipped with all the latest tricks of their trade, may be able to tell us with some precision why people join churches in America in the 1960s; to compare their findings with the situation in the 1860s we have to rely on what they would call much "softer" data.

All the same, the proposition of the demise of the supernatural, or at least of its considerable decline, in the modern world is very plausible in terms of the available evidence. It is to be hoped that more plentiful and more precise evidence will yet be produced, and that there will be greater collaboration between social scientists and historians in this undertaking. But even now we have as good an empirical foundation for the proposition as we do for most generalizations about our world. Whatever the situation may have been in the past, *today* the supernatural as a meaningful reality is absent or remote from the horizons of everyday life of large numbers, very probably of the majority, of people in modern societies, who seem to manage to get along without it quite well. This means that those to whom the supernatural is still, or again, a meaningful reality find themselves in the status of a minority, more precisely, a *cognitive minority*—a very important consequence with very far-reaching implications.

By a cognitive minority I mean a group of people whose view of the world differs significantly from the one generally taken for granted in their society. Put differently, a cognitive minority is a group formed around a body of deviant "knowledge." The quotation marks should be stressed here. The term "knowledge" used within the frame of reference of the sociology of knowledge always refers to what is *taken to be* or *believed as* "knowledge." In other words, the use of the terms is strictly neutral on the question of whether or not the socially held "knowledge" is finally true or false. All human societies are based on "knowledge" in this sense. The sociology of knowledge seeks to understand the different forms of this. The same quotation marks apply to my use of the adjective "cognitive," of course. Instead of saying that societies have bodies of knowledge, we can say that they have cognitive structures. Once more, this in no way implies a judgment of the final validity of these "cognitions." This should be kept in mind whenever the adjective is used in the following argument. Put simply, the sociologist qua sociologist always stays in the role of reporter. He reports that people believe they "know" such and such, and that this belief has such and such consequences. As soon as he ventures an opinion on whether the belief is finally justified, he is jumping out of the role of sociologist. There is nothing wrong with this role change, and I intend to perform it myself in a little while. But one should be clear about what one is doing when.

For better or for worse, men are social beings. Their "sociality" includes what they think, or believe they "know" about the world.[7] Most of what we "know" we have taken on the authority of others, and it is only as others continue to confirm this "knowledge" that it continues to be plausible to us. It is such socially shared, socially taken-for-granted "knowledge" that allows us to move with a measure of confidence through everyday life. Conversely, the plausibility of "knowledge" that is not socially shared, that is challenged by our fellow men, is imperiled, not just in our dealings with others, but much more importantly in our own minds. The status of a cognitive minority is thus invariably an uncomfortable one—not necessarily because the majority is repressive or intolerant, but simply because it refuses to accept the minority's definitions of reality *as* "knowledge." At best, a minority viewpoint is forced to be defensive. At worst, it ceases to be plausible to anyone.

Highly intriguing studies, which it would be unpractical to

review here, have been made of this social dimension of our cognitive life.[8] One example may illustrate its importance. A person coming to America from a culture in which it is part of everyone's "knowledge" that the stars influence human events will, if he expresses this "knowledge" in the United States, soon discover what it means to belong to a cognitive minority. He will be listened to with shocked surprise or tolerant amusement. Attempts may be made to "educate" him, or he may be encouraged to exhibit his exotic notions and thus to play the role of ethnological specimen. Unless he can insulate himself against this massive challenge to his previously taken-for-granted reality (which would presuppose an available group of fellow astrologers to take refuge with), he will soon begin to doubt his challenged "knowledge." There are various ways of coping with doubt. Our cognitive exile could decide to keep his truths to himself—thus depriving them of all social support—or he could try to gain converts; or he could seek for some sort of compromise, perhaps by thinking up "scientific" reasons for the validity of his astrological lore, thus contaminating his reality with the cognitive assumptions of his challengers. Individuals vary in their ability to resist social pressure. The predictable conclusion of the unequal struggle is, however, the progressive disintegration of the plausibility of the challenged "knowledge" in the consciousness of the one holding it. The example may seem loaded—after all, presumably both the writer and the readers of this book "know" that astrology is a lot of nonsense.

To make the point clearer, the example can be reversed. An American stranded in an astrological culture will find his "scientific" view of the world tottering under exactly the same social assaults that undermine astrology in America, and the end result is equally predictable. This is the kind of thing that happens to cultural anthropologists in the field. They call it "culture shock" and cope with it by means of various rituals of detachment (this is the latent psychological function of field procedures), by staying in the company of or at least in communication with fellow outsiders to the culture being studied, and best of all by going home from the field after a relatively brief period of time. The penalty for failure in these efforts to remain outside the situation is "to go native." To be sure, cultural anthropologists like to do this behaviorally ("participant observation") and even emotionally ("empathy"). If they "go native" *cognitively*, however, they will no longer be able to do cultural anthropology. They will have dropped out of the universe of discourse in which such an enterprise is meaningful or even real.

So far, then, we have amplified the proposition concerning the demise of the supernatural in the modern world in two ways: We have conceded the empirical viability of the proposition and we have suggested that such supernaturalists as may still be around will find their beliefs buffeted by very strong social and psychological pressures. Therefore it is hardly surprising that a profound theological crisis exists today. The theologian like every other human being exists in a social milieu. He too is the product of socialization processes. His "knowledge" has been socially acquired, is in need of social support, and is thus vulnerable to social pressures. If the term "supernatural" is understood in the above-mentioned sense, it must be further observed that, at least traditionally, its meaningfulness has been a necessary condition of the theological enterprise. It follows that, in a situation where one may speak of a demise of the supernatural, and *where the theologian himself does so* when he describes the situation, the theological enterprise is confronted with truly formidable difficulties. The theologian more and more resembles a witch doctor stranded among logical positivists—or, of course, a logical positivist stranded among witch doctors. Willy-nilly he is exposed to the exorcisms of his cognitive antagonists. Sooner or later these exorcisms will have their effect in undermining the old certainties in his own mind.

Historical crises are rarely consummated in one dramatic moment. They are contained in processes that extend over varying periods of time and that are experienced in different ways by those affected. As Nietzsche tells us in the famous passage about the "death of God": "This tremendous event is still on its way . . . it has not yet reached the ears of man. Lightning and thunder require time, the light of the stars requires time, deeds require time even after they are done, before they can be seen and heard."[9] It would therefore be extraordinarily naïve to expect the demise of the supernatural to be equally visible from all vantage points of our culture or to be experienced in the same way by all who have taken cognizance of it. There continue to be religious and theological milieux in which the crisis is, at the most, dimly sensed as an external threat in the distance. In other milieux the crisis is beginning to be felt, but is "still on its way." In yet other milieux the crisis is in full eruption as a threat deep inside the fabric of religious practice, faith, and thought. And in some places it is as if the believer or theologian were standing in a landscape of smoldering ruins.

These differences in the perception and absorption of the crisis run across the traditional divisions between the religious groupings of Western culture. But the divisions are still significant in terms of the over-all impact of the crisis. Protestantism has lived with the crisis longest and most intensively, lived with it, that is, as an internal rather than an external cataclysm. This is because Protestant thought has always been particularly open to the spirit of modernity. Very probably this openness has its historical roots not only in an intellectual or spiritual affinity but in the important part that Protestantism actually played in the genesis of the modern world, as Max Weber and others have shown. Be this as it may, one can perceive a major trend of accommodation to modern this-worldliness in Protestant thought for well over a century, beginning as far back as 1799, when Schleiermacher's *Addresses on Religion to Its Cultured Despisers* were first published. The century that followed, extending into the present century up to

World War I, saw the rise to dominance of a theological liberalism whose crucial concern was a cognitive adjustment of Christianity to the (actual or alleged) world view of modernity and one of whose major results was the progressive dismantling of the supernaturalist scaffolding of the Christian tradition. Indeed, the intended audience of Schleiermacher's *Addresses* was prophetic too. Increasingly, Protestant theology has oriented itself by changing coteries of "cultured despisers" of religion, that is, by shifting groups of secularized intellectuals whose respect it solicited and whose cognitive presuppositions it accepted as binding. In other words, Protestant theologians have been increasingly engaged in playing a game whose rules have been dictated by their cognitive antagonists. While this curious vulnerability (not to say lack of character) can probably be explained sociologically, what is interesting here is the over-all result—a profound erosion of the traditional religious contents, in extreme cases to the point where nothing is left but hollow rhetoric. Of late it seems more and more as if the extreme has become the norm.

For a short time, roughly from the end of World War I until shortly after World War II (there are some differences in the duration of this period between Europe and America, and to some extent between denominations), the trend appeared to be about to be reversed. This was the period marked by the ascent of what was variously called neo-Protestantism, dialectical theology, or (most aptly) neo-orthodoxy, ushered in with éclat in 1919 with the publication of Karl Barth's *Epistle to the Romans*. With tremendous passion Barth, particularly in his early work in the 1920s, repudiated all the major assumptions of Protestant liberalism. He called for a return to the classical faith of the Reformation, a faith that, he maintained, was unconditionally based on God's revelation and not on any human reason or experience. In retrospect it is clear that this period was an interruption rather than a reversal of the secularizing trend. It also seems likely that the interlude had a very specific historical and social-psychological foundation, namely the tremendous shocks administered to the self-confidence of the culture in general and its Christian sector in particular by the horrors of war, revolution, and economic disaster. This was, of course, especially true of German-speaking Protestantism and its confrontation with the anti-Christian delirium of Nazism. Theological liberals have gibed that neo-orthodoxy was basically a kind of postwar neurosis, a case of spiritual battle fatigue. This view has a good deal of historical plausibility. It should not surprise us, then, that the "normalization" of society setting in after World War II (in Germany this can be dated quite precisely, and in the context embarrassingly, by the currency reform of 1948) led to a rapid decline of neo-orthodoxy and to the resurgence of various strands of neo-liberalism.

More or less intact milieux of Protestant conservatism still exist, of course. These are typically located on the fringes of urban, middle-class society. They are like besieged fortresses, and their mood tends toward a militancy that only superficially covers an underlying sense of panic. At times, in eruptions of frustrated aggression, the militancy becomes hysterical. Today, the neo-orthodox, who only a few years ago could think of themselves as representing the upsurge of a new Reformation, find themselves dwindling in both numbers and influence. Most of them are elderly veterans of battles that have become unreal to the new generation (such as the battles of German Protestantism in the 1930s), and they are often even more out of touch with what animates the younger theologians than the old-line conservatives who never modified their orthodoxies with the (possibly fatal) prefix "neo-." The theological novelties that have dominated the Protestant scene in the last two decades all seem basically to take up where the older liberalism left off. This is certainly, and in these cases biographically, the case with Paul Tillich and Rudolf Bultmann. Tillich understood the task of theology as one of "correlation," by which he meant the intellectual adjustment of the Christian tradition with philosophical truth. Bultmann proposed a program of what he called "demythologization," a restatement of the biblical message in language free from the supernaturalist notions of ancient man. Both Tillich and Bultmann drew heavily on existentialism (particularly as developed in Germany by Martin Heidegger) for the concepts employed in their efforts to translate Christianity into terms adequate for modern man. The various recent movements of "radical" or "secular" theology have returned even more unambiguously to the old liberalism whether the "cultured despisers" being cognitively embraced are psychoanalysts, sociologists, existentialists, or language analysts.[10] The self-liquidation of the theological enterprise is undertaken with an enthusiasm that verges on the bizarre, culminating in the reduction to absurdity of the "God-is-dead theology" and "Christian atheism." It is no wonder that even those clergy, younger theologians, and, with particular poignancy, theological students who are not simply eager to be "with it" in terms of the latest ideological fashions are afflicted with profound malaise in this situation. The question "What next?" may sometimes be the expression of an intellectual attitude geared to fads and publicity; but it may also be a genuine cry *de profundis*. In the American situation the option of political activity, made morally reasonable by the unspeakable mess of our domestic and international affairs, can serve as a welcome relief, a liberating "leap" from ambiguity to commitment. I do not for one moment wish to disparage this option, but it should be clear from even moderate reflection that the fundamental *cognitive* problem will not be solved in this manner.

The Catholic situation is different, at least in part because Catholicism has viewed the modern world with much more suspicion from the beginning and, as a result, has managed to keep up its cognitive defenses against modernity more effectively and until a much more recent date. Throughout the nineteenth century, while Protestant liberalism carried on its great love affair with the spirit of the age, the basic temper of Catholicism can be described as a magnificent defiance. This temper is exemplified by the figure of Pius IX, whose *Syllabus of Errors* of 1864 condemned, among other modern abominations, the claim that "the Roman Pontiff can and ought to reconcile himself to, and agree with, progress, liberalism and civilization as lately introduced." It was in the same pontificate that the First Vatican Council proclaimed papal infallibility as well as the immaculate conception, in July 1870 in the very teeth of "civilization as lately introduced," which, two months later, marched into Rome in the shape of Victor Emmanuel's army. As late as 1950 (on the very eve of sputnik, as it were) this splendid recalcitrance in the face of modernity manifested itself once more in the proclamation of the dogma of the bodily assumption of Mary into heaven. But that was in the pontificate of Pius XII. The winds of change began to blow more wildly under John XXIII.

It goes without saying that there were undercurrents of accommodation and modernization long before this. The very constitution of the Catholic church, however, provided the means by which these currents could, indeed, be kept *under*. Thus the whole syndrome of secularization, including the demise of the supernatural, could be officially diagnosed as a malady of the world outside the gates. On the inside, the supernaturalist apparatus of mystery and miracle could go on as before—just as long as the defenses (political as well as cognitive) were properly manned, or so it seemed. Such fifth columns within the church as, for instance, the modernist movement around the turn of the century were promptly and effectively repressed. In this particular instance the Freudian allegory of hydraulics is most apt: The repressed impulses, when finally released, threaten to blow off the roof. The pumps, of course, began to gush with Vatican II. The ancient dikes showed punctures. Not that there were no little boys ready and willing to stick their fingers into all the holes—the conservatives were, and did. And now, when all the furniture seems to be swimming out to sea, they can say with some justice, "We told you so."

The theological flux that has engulfed large segments of Catholicism since Vatican II is still very new. There are still sizable islands of immunity, especially in geographical or social areas that are relatively sheltered from modern mass communications (not to speak of literacy). But in Catholic intellectual milieux, the very milieux in which the theological enterprise must be socially rooted, there have of late emerged noises of a fearful modernity sufficient to put the most "radical" Protestant to shame. David Martin, a British sociologist of religion, has described this process with admirable succinctness: "Most Protestant countries in the Anglo-Saxon ambit have been so used to religious vacuity that another cloud of existentialist dust barely disturbs the clarity of their theological vision. But for those only lately inured to clear and distinct ideas like Thomism or to the firm exercise of authority, the effect is startling. Just as Catholics who cease to be conservative often become Marxists so those who cease to be Thomist easily embrace the most extreme existentialist fashion. They are experts at excluding the middle."[11] In other words, in religion as in politics, if one once starts to clobber the opposition, one stops clobbering at one's peril. The peril was predictable. The irony of the situation is that the Catholic liberals, who rank sociology high in their hierarchy of secular revelations, have failed to see the peril. The conservatives, who generally view sociology as one of the more nefarious devilries of modern intellect, smelled the danger signals a mile off. It may well be that conservatives usually have the better sociological noses.

The Jews have experienced the crisis differently. For one thing, Judaism, unlike Christianity, has never developed authoritative and rigorously defined systems of theological propositions. Orthodoxy in Judaism has always been more a matter of practice than of belief. An orthodox Jew can hold any number of perhaps wildly modernistic ideas without necessarily feeling that these are inconsistent with his attitudes regarding family excursions on Saturday or family meals with certain kinds of salami. Thus the efforts of Mordecai Kaplan to "reconstruct" Judaism by getting rid of its entire baggage of traditional supernaturalism, while enraging a goodly number of his fellow rabbis, created less of a storm among American Jews than a comparable program would have, certainly at the time of its initial promulgation in the 1930s, in most Christian milieux. For another thing, Judaism, unlike any Western form of Christianity, has an ethnic dimension, which is closely related to its religious tradition but may also be divorced from it. The modern crisis of Judaism has been closely linked to the so-called problem of Jewish identity, and there have been various strictly secular solutions to this, the most successful having been political Zionism. Nevertheless secularization has plunged Judaism into a dilemma as great as Christianity's. It is all very well to say that Judaism is, above all, a matter of practice. This practice is, however, rooted in a specific cognitive universe without which it is threatened with meaninglessness. The numerous pre- and proscriptions of orthodox Judaism are likely to appear as so many absurdities, unless they remain linked to a world view that includes the supernatural. Lacking this, despite all sorts of traditional loyalties and nostalgias, the whole edifice of traditional piety takes on the character of a museum of religious history. People may like museums, but they are reluctant to live in them. And the secular solutions to the problem of Jewish identity become highly tenuous unless there is *either* anti-Semitic pressure *or* a "natural" Jewish community to which the individual can belong regardless of his religious orientation. The decline of both conditions in contemporary America has produced considerable worries for American Jewish leadership. In Israel, where the second condition pertains, the debates, extending into legal controversy, over the relationship of Jewishness, Judaism, and Israeli nationality indicate the appearance of new variations of the classical problem of identity. In neither country does it seem plausible to exempt Judaism as a religion from the crisis that interests us here.[12]

As we have seen, the crisis is refracted in different ways through the several prisms of religious traditions, but no tradition within the orbit of modern Western societies is exempt from it. A good case can also be made (though not here) that religious traditions in non-Western societies that are undergoing modernization become engulfed in the same crisis, the extent of the crisis keeping pace with the extent of modernization.

In this confrontation between religion and modernity the case of Protestantism is the prototype. Both Catholic and Jewish writers in America have referred to the "Protestantization" of their respective communities, by which they usually mean certain features of their community life (for example, the development of the church as a social center for its congregation, or the emergence of the clergy into public life on certain current issues) that can be attributed to Protestant influence. The term, however, has deeper implications. The case of Protestantism may well serve other religious traditions as a highly instructive example of the impact of the crisis and its various effects. It was Protestantism that first underwent the onslaught of secularization; Protestantism that first adapted itself to societies in which several faiths existed on equal terms, the pluralism may be regarded as a twin phenomenon to secularization,[13] and it was in Protestant theology that the cognitive challenges to traditional supernaturalism were first met and fought through. The Protestant experience has a vicarious quality about it, especially in its assorted miseries. Catholic and Jewish writers, who on occasion are prone to be patronizing about these miseries, might do well to watch the portents and to realize that they are in no way immune to the same perils.

How one predicts the future course of the secularizing trend obviously depends to a large extent on how one explains the origins and the moving forces of the trend to begin with. There are many different theories of the roots of secularization,[14] but whether one sees the process in terms of the history of ideas (listing factors such as the growth of scientific rationalism or the latent secularity of biblical religion itself), or whether one prefers more sociologically oriented theories (with factors such as industrialization, urbanization, or the pluralism of social milieux), it is difficult to see why any of these elements should suddenly reverse themselves. It is more reasonable to assume that a high degree of secularization is a cultural concomitant of modern industrial societies, at least as we now know them, so that abrupt changes in the secularizing trend are not very likely in the foreseeable future. This presupposes what Kahn and Wiener rather nicely call a "surprise-free" world, that is, a world in which present trends continue to unfold without the intrusion of totally new and unexpected factors.

Our "futurologists" themselves seem a little nervous about the notion of "surprise-freeness," and with good reason. One might wonder whether someone equipped with the techniques of modern social science in the late fifteenth century would have been in a position to predict the imminence of the Reformation —or a similarly precocious type in the late first century the coming expansion of Christianity. One of the elements that keeps history from being a complete bore is that it is full of "surprises." At the present time it is easy to envision a number of possible "surprises" that would mean that all bets are off, with regard to secularization or any other present trend—a thermonuclear war devastating much of the world, a complete collapse of the capitalist economic system, permanent racial war in America, and so on. If any of these are in store for us, attempts at prognosis are futile. It would hardly help our understanding to predict the appearance of strange new religions among the wretched survivors of a thermonuclear Armageddon. We lack the data to play through, in the case of religion, what Kahn and Wiener call "canonical variations," that is, possible constellations of "surprise" developments. But despite these limitations, some further observations are possible. We can assume the continuation of the secularizing trend and then proceed to ask what options this leaves for religion and theological thought—options that will, of course, have to be exercised under the conditions of a cognitive minority.

The fundamental option is simple: It is a choice between hanging on to or surrendering cognitive deviance. This choice belongs to the realm of ideas. But it is very important to understand that it has practical social implications.

Choices in real life are rarely pure, but to understand the middle ground it is helpful to imagine the extremes. At one extreme, then, is the option to maintain (or possibly to reconstruct) a supernaturalist position in the teeth of a cognitively antagonistic world. This entails an attitude of the stiff upper lip, a steadfast refusal to "go native," a (literally or otherwise) pontifical insouciance about the opinions of mankind. The theologian with this stance will stick to his trade, supernaturalism and all, and the world (literally or otherwise) be damned. Assuming the continuation of the secularizing trend, this stance is not going to get any easier to maintain. There will be extremely strong social and social-psychological pressures against it. Unless our theologian has the inner fortitude of a desert saint, he has only one effective remedy against the threat of cognitive collapse in the face of these pressures: He must huddle together with like-minded fellow deviants—and huddle very closely indeed. Only in a counter-community of considerable strength does cognitive deviance have a chance to maintain itself. The countercommunity provides continuing therapy against the creeping doubt as to whether, after all, one may not be wrong and the majority right. To fulfill its function of providing social support for the deviant body of "knowledge," the countercommunity must provide a strong sense of solidarity among its members (a "fellowship of the saints" in a world rampant with devils) and it must be quite closed vis-à-vis the outside ("Be not yoked together with un-believers!"). In sum, it must be a kind of ghetto.

People may be forced into ghettos, or they may elect to live in them. It is relevant to recall that Judaism originally created the ghetto as a segregated countercommunity, not because of outside coercion, but because of its own religious necessities. Probably as far back as the Babylonian exile the segregated Jewish community was the social expression (and, one may add, a so-ciologically necessary one) of the separateness, the difference of the Jewish religion. Without the fence of the law, as the rabbis well realized, Judaism could not have survived in the midst of the Gentiles. Inevitably this theological fence had to produce a practical social analogue. But to live in a fenced-in milieu requires strong motivation. In the absence of such motivation, only per-secution or outside force can produce the social conditions nec-essary for the survival of the cognitive deviance.

When people themselves elect to live in this kind of segregation from the larger society we have the phenomenon that sociologists have analyzed as sectarianism. The term "sect" is used in dif-ferent ways in common speech. Sociologically, it means a reli-gious group that is relatively small, in tension with the larger society and closed (one might say "balled up") against it, and that makes very strong claims on the loyalty and solidarity of its members. The choice to persist in defiant cognitive deviance necessarily also entails the choice of sectarian forms of social organization. But people must somehow be motivated to live in such sects. Sometimes this can happen "naturally," if the sec-tarian or ghetto community coincides with ethnic or class barriers set up by the larger society. This happened for a while with Catholicism in the United States, but as the barriers began to come down the sectarian motives declined in the same measure. Sometimes the larger society may be so unattractive that the sectarian underworld has an appeal over and beyond its particular message. This probably helps to account for the period of neo-orthodox ascendancy in European Protestantism. In a world full of Nazis one can be forgiven for being a Barthian.

The trouble with the sectarian option, at least in a "surprise-free" projection of the future, is that such "favorable" circumstances are not very likely to recur. Social mobility and integration are likely to increase, not recede. Modern governments are unlikely to start imposing religious conformity after a long-lasting trend in the opposite direction. Even the most fundamentalist Marxists seem to be losing their taste for religious persecution. The resulting conditions are not only unfavorable to the maintenance of religious monopolies in any sizable segments of the society, they also produce an open market for world views, religious or secular, in which sects have a hard time thriving.[15] In other words, the modern situation is conducive to open systems of "knowledge" in competition and communication with each other, and not to the closed structures in which widely deviant "knowledge" can be cultivated.

The option of cognitive defiance, then, runs into considerable difficulties of "social engineering." To these must be added, in the case of the major Christian groups, a profound aversion to sectarian forms. Christianity has behind it many centuries of universalism and social establishment. The suggestion to go underground, as it were, is unlikely to recommend itself to many churchmen or theologians, least of all in the Catholic camp. The odd sound and indeed literally contradictory meaning of the phrases "Catholic sect" or "sectarian Catholicism" reveal the fundamental spiritual incompatibility.

The polar opposite of defiance is surrender. In this option the cognitive authority and superiority of whatever is taken to be "the *Weltanschauung* of modern man" is conceded with few if any reservations. Modernity is swallowed hook, line, and sinker, and the repast is accompanied by a sense of awe worthy of Holy Communion. Indeed, the sense of injury and incomprehension evinced by modernist theologians whose cognitive celebration is rejected could well be put in the words of the Anglican *Book of Common Prayer*, in the pre-Communion exhortation to negligent parishioners: "Ye know how grievous and unkind a thing it is, when a man hath prepared a rich feast, decked his table with all kind of provision, so that there lacketh nothing but the guests to sit down: and yet they who are called . . . most unthankfully refuse to come." At the moment, of course, there is little reason to complain on this score—the feast lacketh not in attendance.

The basic intellectual task undertaken as a result of this option is one of *translation*. The traditional religious affirmations are translated into terms appropriate to the new frame of reference, the one that allegedly conforms to the *Weltanschauung* of modernity. Different translation grammars have been employed for this purpose, depending on the preferences of the theologians in question as well as their different notions as to the character of the modern *Weltanschauung*. In the cases of Paul Tillich and Rudolf Bultmann, the grammars are variants of existentialism. In the more recent American derivations of "radical" theology, some sort of Jungian psychology, linguistic philosophy, and popular sociology have been used to accomplish the translation. Whatever the differences in method, the result is very similar in all these cases: The supernatural elements of the religious traditions are more or less completely liquidated, and the traditional language is transferred from other-worldly to this-worldly referents. The traditional lore, and in most cases the religious institution in charge of this lore as well, can then be presented as still or again "relevant" to modern man.

It goes without saying that these procedures require a good deal of intellectual contortionism. The major sociological difficulty, however, lies elsewhere. The various forms of secularized theology, unless they are understood as individual intellectual exercises (something against which the ecclesiastical background of most of their protagonists militates), propose various practical pay-offs. Typically, the lay recipient of these blessings will be either a happier person (his existential anxieties assuaged or his archetypal needs fulfilled) or a more effective citizen (usually this means a bigger and better political liberal), or perhaps both. The trouble is that these benefits are also available under strictly secular labels. A secularized Christianity (and, for that matter, a secularized Judaism) has to go to considerable exertion to demonstrate that the religious label, as modified in conformity with the spirit of the age, has anything special to offer. Why should one buy psychotherapy or racial liberalism in a "Christian" package, when the same commodities are available under purely secular and for that very reason even more modernistic labels? The preference for the former will probably be limited to people with a sentimental nostalgia for traditional symbols—a group that, under the influence of the secularizing theologians, is steadily dwindling. For most people, symbols whose content has been hollowed out lack conviction or even interest. In other words, the theological surrender to the alleged demise of the supernatural defeats itself in precisely the measure of its success. Ultimately, it represents the self-liquidation of theology and of the institutions in which the theological tradition is embodied.

Extreme choices are, however, not only relatively rare, they are particularly unlikely to be adopted by sizable institutions with a variety of vested interests in social survival. There may be coteries of intellectuals to whom something like "Christian atheism" has an appeal, but a banner with this strange device is unlikely to be taken up by any of the major churches. Conversely, the extreme of defiant traditionalism is likely to be restricted to smaller groups, typically those whose social location (in "backward" regions, say, or in the lower classes) gives them little interest or stake in the world of modernity. The larger religious groups are rather inclined toward various forms and degrees of *aggiornamento*, that is of limited, controlled accommodation.

Cognitively, this stance involves a bargaining process with modern thought, a surrender of some traditional (which here equals supernatural) items while others are kept.

This was the classical pattern of Protestant theological liberalism. Under new guises it has come to the fore again, in Protestantism since World War II and in Catholicism since Vatican II. While this pattern has the healthiest prospects in terms of social survival values, it has its own troubles too. The main one is a built-in escalation factor—escalation, that is, toward the pole of cognitive surrender. *Aggiornamento* usually arises out of tactical considerations. It is argued that one must modify certain features of the institution or its message because otherwise one will not be able to reach this or that recalcitrant clientele—the intelligentsia, or the working class, or the young. These modifications, however, entail a process of *rethinking*, the end results of which are hard to predict or control. Tactical modifications thus tend to escalate toward genuinely cognitive modifications. At this point the outside challenge becomes a challenge from within. The cognitive antagonist has crept inside the gates and, worse, inside the consciousness of the theologian assigned to guard the gates. The notion that trade promotes understanding is a sound one. When one trades ideas, however, the understanding pushes toward agreement, for those reasons deeply grounded in man's social nature that have been mentioned before. In other words, once one starts a process of cognitive bargaining, one subjects oneself to mutual cognitive contamination. The crucial question then is, Who is the stronger party? If the secularization thesis holds, the stronger party, of course, is the modern world in which the supernatural has become irrelevant. The theologian who trades ideas with the modern world, therefore, is likely to come out with a poor bargain, that is, he will probably have to give far more than he will get. To vary the image, he who sups with the devil had better have a long spoon. The devilry of modernity has its own magic: The theologian who sups with *it* will find his spoon getting shorter and shorter—until that last supper in which he is left alone at the table, with no spoon at all and with an empty plate. The devil, one may guess, will by then have gone away to more interesting company.

Having considered the options and their likely consequences on the "surprise-free" prognosis that the secularizing trend will continue as before, it may be useful now to look briefly at some possible modifications of the trend short of the cataclysmic possibilities in which any prognosis would come to nought. Dean Inge once remarked that a man who marries the spirit of the age soon finds himself a widower. This can be the result of external events, and sometimes happens quite suddenly. For example, as recently as 1965 Harvey Cox in *The Secular City* invited us to celebrate the advent of modern urbanism as if it were some sort of divine revelation. Only a few years later it is difficult to rouse much enthusiasm for *this* particular bit of "timely" wisdom. American cities seem fated to go up in flame in an annual ritual of mad destructiveness and futility. The civil rights movement, which presumably gave Cox confidence in the libertarian future of urban secularity, seems dead as a political force. And that larger city, which is the American polity, has been bled of its moral substance in the war in Vietnam. Right now very few people in America are in a mood to celebrate much of anything in their city. The lesson of this example can be augmented by a look into even the nearest future. It is quite possible that the Vietnamese war will end in the near future, even end abruptly, and that its termination will be followed by policies that come closer to sanity and humaneness. It is also possible that the war will go on for a long time or, even worse, that one Vietnam will follow another in a series of imperial adventures. If "timeliness" is the criterion, how are Christians to follow Cox's admonition to "speak politically"? In the stirring notes of millenarian optimism that marked the early civil rights movement? Or in the apocalyptic mood that seems more appropriate right now? Depending upon how things go, the one or the other option could become obsolete in no time at all. "Relevance" is a very fragile business at best.

It is not only the vagaries and sudden turns of external events that make it so. The organization of our cultural life creates a fragility. Relevance and timeliness are defined for the society at large, primarily by the media of mass communication. These are afflicted with an incurable hunger for novelty. The relevancies they proclaim are, almost by definition, extremely vulnerable to changing fashions and thus of generally short duration. As a result, the theologian (or, of course, any other intellectual) who seeks to be and remain "with it," in terms of mass-communicated and mass-communicable relevance, is predestined to find himself authoritatively put down as irrelevant very soon. Those who consider themselves too sophisticated for mass culture take their cues on relevance and timeliness from an assortment of intellectual cliques, which have their own communications system, characterized by fashions that are more intolerant but hardly more durable than those of the mass media. In this country the maharajas of the world of true sophistication are mainly individuals whose baptism in secularity has been by total immersion. The theologian who wants to take his cues from this source is unlikely even to be recognized short of abject capitulation to the realities taken for granted in these particular circles—realities hardly conducive to the theological enterprise in any form. But even he who is ready for such capitulation should be cautioned. Intellectuals are notoriously haunted by boredom (they like to call this "alienation" nowadays). Our intellectual maharajas are no exception, if only because they mainly talk to each other. There is no telling what outlandish religiosity, even one dripping with savage supernaturalism, may yet arise in these groups, which will once more leave our theologian where he started, on the outside of the cocktail party, looking in.

But let us assume that theological relevance is oriented by

long-term social trends rather than by fleeting fashions, eso- or exoteric. Even here a little caution is in order. There is scattered evidence that secularization may not be as all-embracing as some have thought, that the supernatural, banished from cognitive respectability by the intellectual authorities, may survive in hidden nooks and crannies of the culture. Some, for that matter, are not all that hidden. There continue to be quite massive manifestations of that sense of the uncanny that modern rationalism calls "superstition"—last but not least in the continuing and apparently flourishing existence of an astrological subculture! For whatever reasons, sizable numbers of the specimen "modern man" have not lost a propensity for awe, for the uncanny, for all those possibilities that are legislated against by the canons of secularized rationality.[16] These subterranean rumblings of supernaturalism can, it seems, coexist with all sorts of upstairs rationalism. In a study of American students, 80 per cent of the respondents expressed a "need for religious faith," while only 48 per cent admitted to a belief in God in traditional Judaeo-Christian terms.[17] Even more startling, in a recent opinion poll conducted in western Germany, 68 per cent said that they believed in God—but 86 per cent admitted to praying![18] There are different ways of interpreting such data. They can perhaps be explained quite simply in terms of mankind's chronic illogicality. But perhaps they express a more significant discrepancy between verbal assent to the truisms of modernity and an actual world view of much greater complexity. In this connection the following data give one pause: According to studies made in England, nearly 50 per cent of the respondents had consulted a fortuneteller, one in six believed in ghosts—and one in fifteen claimed to have seen one![19]

I would shy away from any explanations, such as those made in a Jungian vein, in terms of the psychology of religion, that is, in terms of alleged religious "needs" that are frustrated by modern culture and seek an outlet in some way. Empirically, the psychological premises here are very dubious. Theologically, there are few ideas less helpful than the one that religious belief relates to religious need as orgasm does to lust. And it is not unthinkable, after all, that in a world as poorly arranged as this one we may be afflicted with "needs" that are doomed to frustration except in illusion (which, of course, is what Freud thought). However, psychology apart, it is possible to argue that the human condition, fraught as it is with suffering and with the finality of death, demands interpretations that not only satisfy theoretically but give inner sustenance in meeting the crisis of suffering and death. In Max Weber's sense of the term, there is a need, social rather than psychological, for *theodicy*. Theodicy (literally, "justification of God") originally referred to theories that sought to explain how an all-powerful and all-good God can permit suffering and evil in the world. Weber used the term more broadly for any theoretical explanation of the meaning of suffering or evil.

There are, of course, secular theodicies. They fail, however, in interpreting and thus in making bearable the extremes of human suffering. They fail notably in interpreting death. The Marxist case is instructive. The Marxist theory of history does, indeed, provide a kind of theodicy: All things will be made whole in the postrevolutionary utopia. This can be quite comforting to an individual facing death on the barricades. Such a death is meaningful in terms of the theory. But the wisdom of Marxism is unlikely to afford much comfort to an individual facing a cancer operation. The death he faces is strictly meaningless within this (and, indeed, any) frame of reference of theodicy slanted toward this world. These remarks are not, at this point, intended as an argument for the truth of religion. Perhaps the truth is comfortless and without ultimate meaning for human hope. Sociologically speaking, however, the stoicism that can embrace this kind of truth is rare. Most people, it seems, want a greater comfort, and so far it has been religious theodicies that have provided it.

There are therefore some grounds for thinking that, at the very least, pockets of supernaturalist religion are likely to survive in the larger society. As far as the religious communities are concerned, we may expect a revulsion against the more grotesque extremes of self-liquidation of the supernaturalist traditions. It is a fairly reasonable prognosis that in a "surprise-free" world the global trend of secularization will continue. An impressive rediscovery of the supernatural, in the dimensions of a mass phenomenon, is not in the books. At the same time, significant enclaves of supernaturalism within the secularized culture will also continue. Some of these may be remnants of traditionalism, of the sort that sociologists like to analyze in terms of cultural lag. Others may be new groupings, possible locales for a rediscovery of the supernatural. Both types will have to organize themselves in more or less sectarian social forms. The large religious bodies are likely to continue their tenuous quest for a middle ground between traditionalism and *aggiornamento*, with both sectarianism and secularizing dissolution nibbling away at the edges. This is not a dramatic picture, but it is more likely than the prophetic visions of either the end of religion or a coming age of resurrected gods.

If my aim here were primarily sociological analysis or prognosis, this would be the end of the argument. Since this is not the case in this book, the preceding is in the nature of preliminary discussion. It is intended to delineate some facets of the situation within which thinking about religion must take place today. I am concerned with the religious questions themselves, on the level of truth rather than timeliness. I also contend (as I will explain next) that the sociological perspective on these questions can yield a little more than a diagnosis of the present situation. No one, to be sure, can think about religion or anything else in sovereign independence of his situation in time and space. The history of human thought demonstrates rather clearly, however, that it is possible to go some way in asking questions of truth while disregarding the spirit of an age, and even to arrive at answers that contradict this spirit. Genuine timeliness means sensitivity to one's socio-historical starting point, *not* fatalism about one's possible destination. What follows, then, is based on the belief that it is possible to liberate oneself to a considerable degree from the taken-for-granted assumptions of one's time. This belief has as its correlate an ultimate indifference to the majority or minority status of one's view of the world, an indifference that is equally removed from the exaltation of being fully "with it" and from the arrogance of esotericism. Perhaps this indifference also has an element of contempt for the emotional satisfactions of either stance.

2
The Perspective of Sociology: Relativizing the Relativizers

Knowledge can be cultivated for its own sake; it can also have very definite existential consequences. It is possible to make the case that existentially (that is, in terms of the individual's existence in the world) true knowledge leads to experiences of ecstasy—of *ek-stasis*, a standing outside of the taken-for-granted routines of everyday life. Bodies and modes of knowledge differ, both in the degree to which they are conducive to such ecstasy and in the character of the ecstasy they provide. There are kinds of knowledge that appear to be quite timeless in this respect; for example, the knowledge of the tragic poet. We can turn from the daily newspaper to Aeschylus or Shakespeare and discover that the insights of the tragedians actually pertain to the events of the day—and the ecstasy thus achieved can, indeed, be a terrifying one.

There are other kinds of knowledge that provide ecstasies of a more timely character. For example, the discovery of the complexity of each individual's subjectivity that gave birth to the novel as a literary form in the modern West is timely and time-bound in a quite different way. We can be moved to ecstasy by Shakespeare, and the Elizabethans could be so moved by Aeschylus, but it is very doubtful that the ecstatic insights of Balzac or Dostoyevsky could have been grasped in the sixteenth century. Conversely, modern Western man appears to have practically lost the capacity to comprehend, let alone to replicate, the ecstatic condition that the practices of various religious cults provided for their members throughout most of previous human history.

Theological thought, which is in the ecstasy business almost by definition, is inevitably affected by the kinds of knowledge that bring about the peculiar ecstasies of the time—regardless of whether these ecstasies are true or false ones by some extraneous criteria of validity, and pretty much regardless of whether theological thought seeks out or resists the same ecstasies. The sociological reasons for this have already been discussed. Another reason is the intrinsic human propensity for unified thought. Honest, sustained reflection recoils from cognitive schizophrenia. It seeks to unify, to reconcile, to understand how one thing taken as truth relates to another so taken. In the history of Christian thought each age has presented its own peculiar challenges to the theologian. Our own age differs only in the acceleration in the sequence of challenges. Not surprisingly, the theologian in our situation is haunted by a sense of vertigo, though he is hardly alone in this affliction.

Marx, in a pun on the German meaning of the name Feuerbach, once said that anyone doing serious philosophy in that time would first have to pass through the "fiery brook" of Feuerbach's thought. Today the sociological perspective constitutes the "fiery brook" through which the theologian must pass—or, perhaps more accurately, ought to pass. It is sociological thought, and most acutely the sociology of knowledge, that offers the specifically contemporary challenge to theology. Theology can, of course, ignore this challenge. It is always possible to avoid challenges, sometimes for a long time. It might be argued, for example, that Hindu thought has managed to avoid the challenge of Buddhism for some twenty-five hundred years. All the same, there are challenges that one avoids at a peril—not necessarily a practical one, but a peril to the integrity of one's thought. In this particular case, because of the crisis discussed previously, avoiding the challenge of sociology will almost certainly have nefarious practical as well as cognitive consequences.

In a broad sense of the term, this is the latest embodiment of the challenge of modern scientific thought. Seen in this context, sociology is simply the most recent in a series of scientific disciplines that have profoundly challenged theology. The physical sciences were probably first in the line of attack, and it is they that first occur to most people when a scientific challenge to theology is mentioned. People think of Copernicus and Galileo, of the challenge to the cosmology of the Middle Ages, particularly to the central position in the universe it assigned to men and man's earth, and, more recently, of the rationally explicable universe of modern physics, in which the "religious hypothesis" becomes increasingly unnecessary to explain reality. However valid the actual conflict between theology and the physical sciences may or may not be, there is no doubt that such a conflict has been profoundly believed to exist, and the over-all effect of this belief has been related to what Max Weber aptly called the disenchantment of the world.

The revolution in biology during the nineteenth century further aggravated the challenge. If Copernicus dethroned man cosmologically, Darwin dethroned him even more painfully biologically. It has been fashionable to relish these metaphysical humiliations of man and to look with superior amusement at the efforts of the backward souls who tried to resist accepting them. Backward they may have been, but hardly amusing. The joke, if anything, is on us. In that case, it is a grim joke. There is really nothing very funny about finding oneself stranded, alone, in a remote corner of a universe bereft of human meaning—nor about the idea that this fate is the outcome of the mindless massacre that Darwin, rather euphemistically, called natural selection. My own sympathies, I must confess, are with the pathetic rear-guard action of William Jennings Bryan rather than with the insipid progress-happiness of Clarence Darrow—an admirable man in many ways, but one dense enough sincerely to believe that a Darwinist view of man could serve as a basis for his opposition to capital punishment.

Contrary to the popular assumptions, I would, however, argue that the physical sciences' challenges to the theology have been *relatively* mild. They have challenged certain literal interpretations of the Bible, such as the belief that the universe was created in seven literal days or that the human race is literally descended from Adam. But such beliefs can, after all, be plausibly interpreted as not touching upon the essence of faith. More serious is that general disenchantment of the world mentioned before, but the very sense of abandonment this brings about can also become a motive for passionate theological affirmations—as the examples of Pascal and Kierkegaard demonstrate. The challenges of the human sciences, on the other hand, have been more critical, more dangerous to the essence of the theological enterprise. Sociology's two important predecessors were, successively, history and psychology. It was historical scholarship, especially as it developed in the nineteenth century, that first threatened to undermine theology at its very roots. Its challenge, too, began with details that could more or less plausibly be dismissed as trivial—the discovery of different sources for biblical books that had been canonized as unities, or of inconsistencies in the several accounts of the life of Jesus. All these details, however, came to add up to something much more serious—a pervasive sense of the historical character of *all* elements of the tradition, which significantly weakened the latter's claims to uniqueness and authority. Put simply, historical scholarship led to a perspective in which even the most sacrosanct elements of religious tradition came to be seen as *human products*. Psychology deepened this challenge, because it suggested that the production could be not only seen but explained. Rightly or wrongly, psychology after Freud suggested that religion was a gigantic projection of human needs and desires—a suggestion all the more sinister because of the unedifying character of these needs and desires, and finally sinister because of the allegedly unconscious mechanisms of the projection process. Thus history and psychology together plunged theology into a veritable vortex of relativizations. The resulting crisis in credibility has engulfed the theological enterprise *in toto*, not merely this or that detail of interpretation.

This is not the place for a critique of the final validity of these challenges. I, for one, take the claims of history more seriously than those of psychology. Be this as it may, the challenge of sociology can be seen as a further intensification of the crisis. The historical nature and product-character, and thus the relativity rather than absolutism, of the religious traditions becomes even more transparent as the social dynamics of their historical production is understood. And the notion of projection becomes much more plausible in its sociological rather than its psychological form, because the former is simpler and more readily verifiable in ordinary, "conscious" experience. Sociology, it may be said, raises the vertigo of relativity to its most furious pitch, posing a challenge to theological thought with unprecedented sharpness.

What are the dimensions of this challenge?

The more obvious dimension is that sociological research gives the theologian a sense of his own minority status in contemporary society. One can, of course, maintain that, here as elsewhere, sociology simply belabors what everyone knows already. After all, the decline of religion in the modern world had been noted, hailed, and bewailed before any sociologists started to investigate the matter. Nevertheless there is a difference between very general, unsubstantiated observations about the alleged spirit of the age and the kind of sober specific data that sociology habitually digs up. For example, it had certainly been known for a long time that the big city is not conducive to traditional piety. But careful statistical data on this subject, such as those accumulated by Gabriel LeBras in his studies of Catholic practice in France, have quite a different shock effect. This was expressed dramatically in LeBras' well-known statement that a certain railroad station in Paris appears to have a magical quality, for rural migrants seem to be changed from practicing to non-practicing Catholics the very moment they set foot in it.

It is very hard to estimate the over-all effect of sociological information as it is diffused in a certain milieu—in this case to judge how important such information has been in the radical rethinking of its own position that has been going on in French Catholicism since World War II. It is obvious, however, that such data as those of LeBras and his school give an altogether different dimension, namely one of scientific verifiability, to such statements as the one that France is in fact mission territory—a statement that was, among other things, influential in starting the worker-priest movement.[20] To take another example, it has probably been common knowledge for a long time that American Protestant ministers were careful of the views of their congregations and that this cautiousness increased with the degree of their professional success. But it is still rather shocking when this fact is brought out with careful documentation, as was done in a study of ministers in the racial crisis in Little Rock.[21]

The shock effect is often unintended. It can begin with very modest, practical questions. A minister, say, wants to find out how well he is getting across to his congregation in his sermons. He decides on a little do-it-yourself sociological research and hands out a questionnaire. The answers come back and show that the greater part of the congregation do not seem to have heard his preaching at all. They agree and disagree, on the questionnaire, with things he never said. This has really happened, by the way, and it is not hard to see that such information would be greatly disturbing to a minister. Let us assume that his curiosity is stirred more deeply now and he proceeds with his research activities. He might next discover that what many in his congregation mean by religion has very little relationship to what he means or to the denominational tradition to which the congregation claims allegiance. He might also find that his own role is understood by members of the congregation in a way that is diametrically opposed to his self-understanding. He thinks he is preaching the gospel, they believe he is providing moral instruction for their children. He wants to have an impact on their social and political beliefs, they want him to stay away from these and edify their family life. And so on. What began with some practical questions on how to be a more effective minister ends with information that puts in question the whole business of ministry and church. Variations of such a process of increasingly alarming insights are far from uncommon in America today and have contributed to the over-all nervousness of the clergy.

There is a certain cruel irony in this, especially in view of the fact that a good deal of the work in the sociology of religion begins as market research undertaken on behalf of religious organizations. The lesson, perhaps, is that one calls on the sociologist at one's peril. One may do so, initially, for the most pragmatic reasons, simply wanting to get information that will be useful in the planning and execution of institutional policies. One may find that, without anyone's (including the sociologist's) desiring it, the information that emerges subverts some basic presuppositions of the institution itself. One is tempted to suggest that sociologists offering their services to institutional bureaucracies pronounce a loud *caveat emptor* before they start working.

There is, however, a more profound dimension to the challenge of sociology to theological thought. This is the dimension of the sociology of knowledge.[22] Its challenge to theological thought lies in its ability to provide a kind of *answer* to the problem of relativity. The answer, though, is not exactly comforting, at least not at first blush.

The sociology of knowledge, a subdiscipline of sociology that began in Germany in the 1920s and was made familiar to English-speaking sociologists through the writings of Karl Mannheim, is concerned with studying the relationship between human thought and the social conditions under which it occurs. Its basic relevance to the subject at hand can be illustrated fairly easily by explaining the concept of plausibility structures.

One of the fundamental propositions of the sociology of knowledge is that the plausibility, in the sense of what people actually find credible, of views of reality depends upon the social support these receive. Put more simply, we obtain our notions about the world originally from other human beings, and these notions continue to be plausible to us in a very large measure because others continue to affirm them. There are some exceptions to this—notions that derive directly and instantaneously from our own sense experience—but even these can be integrated into meaningful views of reality only by virtue of social processes. It is, of course, possible to go against the social consensus that surrounds us, but there are powerful pressures (which manifest themselves as psychological pressures within our own consciousness) to conform to the views and beliefs of our fellow men. It is in conversation, in the broadest sense of the word, that we build up and keep going our view of the world. It follows that this view will depend upon the continuity and consistency of such conversation, and that it will change as we change conversation partners.

We all exist within a variety of social networks or conversational fabrics, which are related in often complex and sometimes contradictory ways with our various conceptions of the universe. When we get to the more sophisticated of these conceptions, there are likely to be organized practices designed to still doubts and prevent lapses of conviction. These practices are called therapies. There are also likely to be more or less systematized explanations, justifications, and theories in support of the conceptions in question. These sociologists have called legitimations.

For example, every society, including our own, organizes the sexual life of its members. Some sexual practices are permitted and even sanctified, others are forbidden and execrated. If all goes well (and that generally means if there are no failures in the socialization of individuals) people will do what they are supposed to do in this area and stay away from the tabu possibilities. The males will, say, marry the women they desire most and refrain from sleeping with each other. But not everything goes well all the time. Occasionally, somebody slips from the straight and narrow path. Society may punish him for this, using the various mechanisms that sociologists call social controls; it may also seek to "help" him. The therapeutic or "helping" agencies will point out his errors and offer him a way of coming back into the fold. In our society, there is a vast network of psychotherapists, counselors, and social workers with just this function. Even when things go well, however, people sometimes ask questions. They want explanations for the moral imperatives that society inflicts on them. These explanations, or legitimations, are designed to convince people that what they are being told to do is not only the prudent thing, but also the only right and salutary one. Many psychologists have performed this trick by identifying socially enjoined sexual behavior with "mental health." In a social situation containing all these therapeutic and legitimating defenses it becomes quite plausible, at least most of the time, to get married and to abhor homosexuality. It would be very different if a society defined "normality" in a different way and imposed this other definition on people. In other words, the plausibility of this or that conception of what is sexually "normal" depends upon specific social circumstances. When we add up all these factors—social definitions of reality, social relations that take these for granted, as well as the supporting therapies and legitimations—we have the total plausibility structure of the conception in question.

Thus each conception of the world of whatever character or content can be analyzed in terms of its plausibility structure, because it is only as the individual remains within this structure that the conception of the world in question will remain plausible to him. The strength of this plausibility, ranging from unquestioned certitude through firm probability to mere opinion, will be directly dependent upon the strength of the supporting structure. This dynamics pertains irrespective of whether, by some outside observer's criteria of validity, the notions thus made plausible are true or false. The dynamics most definitely pertains to any religious affirmations about the world because these affirmations are, by their very nature, incapable of being supported by our own sense experience and therefore heavily dependent upon social support.

Each plausibility structure can be further analyzed in terms of its constituent elements—the specific human beings that "inhabit" it, the conversational network by which these "inhabitants" keep the reality in question going, the therapeutic practices and rituals, and the legitimations that go with them. For example, the maintenance of the Catholic faith in the consciousness of the individual requires that he maintain his relationship to the plausibility structure of Catholicism. This is, above all, a community of Catholics in his social milieu who continually support this faith. It will be useful if those who are of the greatest emotional significance to the individual (the ones whom George Herbert Mead called significant others) belong to this supportive community—it does not matter much if, say, the individual's dentist is a non-Catholic, but his wife and his closest personal friends had better be. Within this supportive community there will then be an ongoing conversation that, explicitly and implicitly, keeps a Catholic world going. Explicitly, there is affirmation, confirmation, reiteration of Catholic notions about reality. But there is also an implicit Catholicism in such a community. After all, in everyday life it is just as important that some things can silently be taken for granted as that some things are reaffirmed in so many words. Indeed, the most fundamental assumptions about the world are commonly affirmed by implication—they are so "obvious" that there is no need to put them into words. Our individual, then, operates within what may be called a specifically Catholic conversational apparatus, which, in innumerable ways, each day confirms the Catholic world that he coinhabits with his significant others. If all these social mechanisms function properly, his Catholicism will be as "natural" to him as the color of his hair or his belief in the law of gravity. He will, indeed, be the happy possessor of an *anima naturaliter christiana*, a "naturally Christian soul."

Such flawlessness in the plausibility structure is unlikely. For this reason, the supportive community (in this instance, the institutional church) provides specific practices, rituals, and legitimations that maintain the faith over and beyond its basic maintenance by a Catholic social milieu. This, of course, includes the whole body of pious practices, from the formal sacraments to the private reassurance rites (such as prayer) recommended to the individual. It also includes the body of knowledge (in the Catholic case, vast in volume and of immense sophistication) that provides explanation and justification for each detail of religious life and belief. And in this instance, of course, there is a staff of highly trained experts as well, who mediate the therapeutic and legitimating machinery to the individual. The details of all of this vary in different circumstances, especially as between a situation in which the plausibility structure is more or less coextensive with the individual's over-all social experience (that is, where Catholics constitute the majority) and a situation in which the plausibility structure exists as a deviant enclave within the individual's larger society (that is, where Catholics are a cognitive minority). But the essential point is that the plausibility of Catholicism hinges upon the availability of these social processes.

It may be objected that this has, in some way, always been known, certainly by Catholic thinkers. One may even say that the formula *extra ecclesiam nulla salus* ("there is no salvation outside the church") expresses the same insight in different language. A moment's reflection will, however, indicate that more is involved than a change of language—and, indeed, most theologians would recoil from a translation of the formula into the proposition "no plausibility without the appropriate plausibility structure." Why? Because the translated version offers an *explanation* of belief that divests the specific case of its uniqueness and authority. The mystery of faith now becomes scientifically graspable, practically repeatable, and generally applicable. The magic disappears as the mechanisms of plausibility generation and plausibility maintenance become transparent. The community of faith is now understandable as a *constructed entity*—it has been constructed in a specific human history, by human beings. Conversely, it can be dismantled or reconstructed by the use of the same mechanisms. Indeed, a would-be founder of a religion can be given a sociological blueprint for the fabrication of the necessary plausibility structure—and this blueprint will contain essentially the same basic elements that have gone into the making of the Catholic community of faith. The formula, once an affirmation of unique authority, thus becomes a general rule. It is applicable to Catholics, Protestants, Theravada Buddhists, Communists, vegetarians, and believers in flying saucers. In other words, the theologian's world has become *one world among many*—a generalization of the problem of relativity that goes considerably beyond the dimensions of the problem as previously posed by historical scholarship. To put it simply: History posits the problem of relativity as *a fact*, the sociology of knowledge as *a necessity of our condition*.

If my purpose here were to upset theologians, this point could be elaborated at great length. Since my purpose is to comfort them, I will simply hope that the point has been made sufficiently clear, that enough has been said to justify the suspicion that sociology is the dismal science par excellence of our time, an intrinsically debunking discipline that should be most congenial to nihilists, cynics, and other fit subjects for police surveillance. Both theological and political conservatives have long suspected just this, and their aversion to sociology is based on a sound instinct for survival. I am not interested at the moment in pursuing the question of whether sociology should, in a well-run society, be forbidden as a corruption of the young and as inimical to good order (Plato, I'm sure, would have thought so). As far as the challenge to theological thought is concerned, however, there are unexpected redeeming features to the sociologist's dismal revelations, and it is these that concern me in the present undertaking.

One cannot throw a sop to the dragon of relativity and then go about one's intellectual business as usual, although Max Scheler, the founder of the sociology of knowledge, tried to do just that. In the sphere of theological thought a similar effort has been made in the distinction, particularly dear to the neo-orthodox camp, between "religion" and "Christian faith"[23]: "Religion" falls under all the relativizing categories that anybody can think up, while "Christian faith" is supposed to be somehow immune from all this, because it is a gift of God's grace rather than a product of man and therefore provides a firm ground from which to survey the quicksands of relativity. One of the most ingenious presentations of this approach can be found in Karl Barth's introduction to Feuerbach.[24] Variations of it lie in such distinctions as the one between "profane history" and "salvation history" (long a cherished Protestant dichotomy), or, more recently, between *Historie* and *Geschichte* (a legerdemain of the Bultmann school that, alas, loses much of its persuasiveness in any language but German).

"Profane history" refers to the ordinary course of events, as it can be studied by the historian; "sacred history" is the story of God's acts in the world, which can be grasped only in the perspective of faith. *Historie* refers to actual historical events, while *Geschichte* refers to occurrences in the existence of the believing individual for which the historical events serve as some sort of symbol. For instance, the historian may find out all sorts of things about Jesus of Nazareth. All these historical findings, however, are supposed to be finally irrelevant, because only faith can grasp that this Jesus is Christ, or because the really important thing is not the historical Jesus but the Christ experienced in the existence of the believing Christian. The reason why this sort of reasoning won't do is twofold: First, the differentiation is meaningless to the empirical investigator—"Christian faith" is simply another variant of the phenomenon "religion," "salvation history" of the historical phenomenon as such, and so forth. The differentiation presupposes a prior exit from the empirical sphere, and therefore it cannot be used to solve a problem arising within that sphere. Second, the firm ground is given by God, "by grace alone," and not achievable by man, which leaves us singularly unedified if we are not already convinced we are standing on this ground, for then, inevitably, we must ask for directions on how to get there. Such directions are not forthcoming in this theological approach, and cannot be by its very logic. This kind of effort to solve the problem of relativity curiously repeats the old Calvinist doctrine of election—you don't get there unless you start from there. It follows that those of us who are lacking in this particular sense of election must either resign ourselves to intellectual damnation or look for another method.

Any such method will have to include a willingness to see the relativity business through to its very end. This means giving up any *a priori* immunity claims (be it in the aforementioned neo-orthodox sense, or in the older liberal manner of trying to allow the relativizing dragon "thus far, but no farther"). It seems, however, that when the operation is completed a rather strange thing happens. When everything has been subsumed under the relativizing categories in question (those of history, of the sociology of knowledge, or what-have-you), the question of truth reasserts itself in almost pristine simplicity. Once we know that all human affirmations are subject to scientifically graspable socio-historical processes, *which affirmations are true and which are false*? We cannot avoid the question any more than we can return to the innocence of its pre-relativizing asking. This loss of innocence, however, makes for the difference between asking the question before and after we have passed through the "fiery brook."

The point can be illustrated by examining recent "radical" or "secular" theology, which takes as both its starting point and its final criterion the alleged consciousness of modern man. It then proceeds to relativize religious tradition by assigning it, in part or as a whole, to a consciousness that is now passé, "no longer possible to us," and to translate it, partially or wholly, into terms that are supposedly consonant with the alleged modern consciousness. An important example of this is Rudolf Bultmann's "demythologization" program, which begins with the premise that no one who uses electricity and listens to the radio can any longer believe in the miracle world of the New Testament and ends by translating key elements of the Christian tradition into the categories of existentialism. Essentially the same procedure characterizes all theologians of this tendency, though they vary in method (some, for instance, preferring linguistic philosophy or Jungian psychology to existentialism).

I am not concerned for the moment with either the viability of the translation process or the empirical validity of the premise about modern man, but rather with a hidden *double standard*, which can be put quite simply: The *past*, out of which the tradition comes, is relativized in terms of this or that socio-historical analysis. The *present*, however, remains strangely immune from relativization. In other words, the New Testament writers are seen as afflicted with a false consciousness rooted in their time, but the contemporary analyst takes the consciousness of *his* time as an unmixed intellectual blessing. The electricity- and radio-users are placed intellectually above the Apostle Paul.

This is rather funny. More importantly, in the perspective of the sociology of knowledge, it is an extraordinarily one-sided way of looking at things. What was good for the first century is good for the twentieth. The world view of the New Testament writers was constructed and maintained by the same kind of social processes that construct and maintain the world view of contemporary "radical" theologians. Each has its appropriate plausibility structure, its plausibility-maintaining mechanisms. If this is understood, then the appeal to *any* alleged modern consciousness loses most of its persuasiveness—unless, of course, one can bring oneself to believe that modern consciousness is indeed the embodiment of superior cognitive powers. Some people can manage this with respect to modern philosophers or psychologists. It is hard to carry off such a feat of faith with respect to the average consumer of electricity and modern *Weltanschauung*. One has the terrible suspicion that the Apostle Paul may have been one-up cognitively, after all. As a result of such considerations an important shift takes place in the argument on the alleged demise of the supernatural in contemporary society. The empirical presuppositions of the argument can be left intact. In other words, it may be conceded that there is in the modern world a certain type of consciousness that has difficulties with the supernatural. The statement remains, however, on the level of socio-historical diagnosis. The diagnosed condition is *not* thereupon elevated to the status of an absolute criterion; the contemporary situation is not immune to relativizing analysis. We may say that contemporary consciousness is such and such; we are left with the question of whether we will assent to it. We may agree, say, that contemporary consciousness is incapable of conceiving of either angels or demons. We are still left with the question of whether, possibly, both angels and demons go on existing despite this incapacity of our contemporaries to conceive of them.

One (perhaps literally) redeeming feature of sociological perspective is that relativizing analysis, in being pushed to its final consequence, bends back upon itself. The relativizers are relativized, the debunkers are debunked—indeed, relativization itself is somehow liquidated. What follows is *not*, as some of the early sociologists of knowledge feared, a total paralysis of thought. Rather, it is a new freedom and flexibility in asking questions of truth.

As far as the contemporary religious crisis is concerned, the sociology of knowledge can go further than stating this general principle. It can throw light on the causes of the credibility crisis of religion today; that is, it can relativize the relativizers in much more specific terms, by showing up the salient features of *their* plausibility structure. The most important feature to grasp here is that of modern *pluralism*, by which I mean, in this context, any situation in which there is more than one world view available to the members of a society, that is, a situation in which there is competition between world views.[25]

As I have tried to show, world views remain firmly anchored in subjective certainty to the degree that they are supported by consistent and continuous plausibility structures. In the case of optimal consistency and continuity, they attain the character of unquestioned and unquestionable certitudes. Societies vary in their capacity to provide such firm plausibility structures. As a general rule of thumb, one can say that the capacity steadily diminishes as one gets closer to modern industrial societies. A primitive tribe does much better than an ancient city. The latter, however, is still far better equipped to produce certitudes than our own social formations. Modern societies are, by their very nature, highly differentiated and segmented, while at the same time allowing for a very high degree of communication between their segmented subsocieties. The reasons for this, while complex, are not at all mysterious. They result from the degree of division of labor brought about by industrial forms of production, and from the patterns of settlement, social stratification, and communication engendered by industrialism. The individual experiences these patterns in terms of differentiated and segmented processes of socialization, which in most cases begin in early childhood. As he grows older he finds he must play many different roles, sometimes quite discrepant ones, and must segregate some of these roles from each other, since they are not all equally appropriate to the different parts of his social life. And, as a result of all this, he comes to maintain an inner detachment or distance with regard to some of these roles—that is, he plays some of them tongue in cheek. For example, in his family he is forced to conform to the manners and morals of middle-class life, while in the company of his contemporaries he is pressured to disregard these "square" characteristics. As long as he associates with both his family and his contemporaries, he will then play highly discrepant roles at different times. If he identifies his "real" self with his family, he will "only superficially" conform to the mores of his contemporaries; if, as is more likely, he more fully identifies with the latter, he will "only play along" with his family. In either case there will be some roles that are performed tongue in cheek, "insincerely," "superficially"—that is, with inner detachment.

Inevitably, this leads to a situation in which most plausibility structures are partial and therefore tenuous. They organize only a part of the individual's world and lack the compelling character of structures taken to be "natural," inevitable, self-evident. Most individuals in primitive or archaic societies lived in social institutions (such as tribe, clan, or even polis) that embraced just about all the significant relationships they had with other people. The modern individual exists in a plurality of worlds, migrating back and forth between competing and often contradictory plausibility structures, each of which is weakened by the simple fact of its involuntary coexistence with other plausibility structures. In addition to the reality-confirming significant others, there are always and everywhere "those others," annoying disconfirmers, disbelievers—perhaps the modern nuisance par excellence.

This pluralization of socially available worlds has been of particular importance for religion, again for far from mysterious reasons, the most decisive being the Protestant Reformation and its subsidiary schisms. It is this pluralization, rather than some mysterious intellectual fall from grace, that I see as the most important cause of the diminishing plausibility of religious traditions. It is relatively easy, sociologically speaking, to be a Catholic in a social situation where one can readily limit one's significant others to fellow Catholics, where indeed one has little choice in the matter, and where all the major institutional forces are geared to support and confirm a Catholic world. The story is quite different in a situation where one is compelled to rub shoulders day by day with every conceivable variety of "those others," is bombarded with communications that deny or ignore one's Catholic ideas, and where one has a terrible time even finding some quiet Catholic corners to withdraw into. It is very, very difficult to be cognitively *entre nous* in modern society, especially in the area of religion. This simple sociological fact, and not some magical inexorability of a "scientific" world outlook, is at the basis of the religious plausibility crisis.

The same fact goes far to explain why it is "no longer possible" to believe in the miracles of the New Testament, or in much of anything religiously. Religious affirmations percolate from the level of taken-for-granted certainty to the level of mere belief, opinion, or (a term that eloquently expresses what goes on here) "religious preference." The pluralistic situation not only allows the individual a choice, it forces him to choose. By the same token, it makes religious certainty very hard to come by. It is instructive to recall that the literal meaning of the word *haeresis* is "choice." In a very real sense, every religious community in the pluralistic situation becomes a "heresy," with all the social and psychological tenuousness that the term suggests. In other words, the contemporary radio-user is not inhibited in his capacity for faith by the scientific knowledge and technology that produced his radio. Very likely, he hasn't the first idea of these, and couldn't care less. But he is inhibited by the multiplicity of ideas and notions about the world that his radio, along with other communications media, plunges him into. And while we may understand and sympathize with his predicament, there is no reason whatever to stand in awe of it.

In short, the perspective of sociology, particularly of the sociology of knowledge, can have a definitely liberating effect. While other analytic disciplines free us from the dead weight of the past, sociology frees us from the tyranny of the present. Once we grasp our own situation in sociological terms, it ceases to impress us as an inexorable fate. Of course, we still cannot magically jump out of our own skins. The forces of our situation work on us even if we understand them, because we are social beings and continue to be even when we become sociologists. But we gain at least a measure of liberation from the taken-for-granted certitudes of our time. The German historian Ranke said that "each age is immediate to God," intending thereby to reject the vulgar progressivism that sees one's own moment in history as history's pinnacle. The perspective of sociology increases our ability to investigate whatever truth each age may have discovered in its particular "immediacy to God."

While this, I think, is a considerable intellectual gain, I would like to go further, to suggest that the entire view of religion as a human product or projection may once again be inverted, and that in such an inversion lies a viable theological method in response to the challenge of sociology. If I am right in this, what could be in the making here is a gigantic joke on Feuerbach.

Feuerbach regarded religion as a gigantic projection of man's own being, that is, as essentially man writ large. He therefore proposed reducing theology to anthropology, that is, explaining religion in terms of its underlying human reality. In doing this, Feuerbach took over Hegel's notion of dialectics, but profoundly changed its significance. The concept of dialectics, in Hegel as elsewhere, refers to a reciprocal relation between a subject and its object, a "conversation" between consciousness and whatever is outside consciousness. Hegel's notion of this was first developed in a theological context, the "conversation" was ultimately one between man and God. With Feuerbach, it was a "conversation" between man and man's own productions. Put differently, instead of a dialogue between man and a superhuman reality, religion became a sort of human monologue.

A good case could be made that not only Marx's and Freud's treatment of religion, but the entire historical-psychological-sociological analysis of religion phenomena since Feuerbach has been primarily a vast elaboration of the same conception and the same procedure. A sociological theory of religion, particularly if it is undertaken in the framework of the sociology of knowledge, pushes to its final consequences the Feuerbachian notion of religion as a human projection, that is, as a scientifically graspable producer of human history.[26]

It is relevant to keep in mind that Feuerbach, Marx, and Freud all inverted the original Hegelian dialectic. Their opponents regarded the inversion as standing the dialectic on its head, while their protagonists conceived of it as putting the dialectic back on its feet. The choice of image obviously depends on one's ultimate assumptions about reality. It is logically possible, however, that *both* perspectives may coexist, each within its particular frame of reference. What appears as a human projection in one may appear as a reflection of divine realities in another. The logic of the first perspective does not preclude the possibility of the latter.

An analogy may be useful in illustrating this point. If there is any intellectual enterprise that appears to be a pure projection of human consciousness it is mathematics. A mathematician can be totally isolated from any contact with nature and still go on about his business of constructing mathematical universes, which spring from his mind as pure creations of human intellect. Yet the most astounding result of modern natural science is the reiterated discovery (quite apart from this or that mathematical formulation of natural processes) that nature, too, is in its essence a fabric of mathematical relations. Put crudely, the mathematics that man projects out of his own consciousness somehow corresponds to a mathematical reality that is external to him, and which indeed his consciousness appears to reflect. How is this possible? It is possible, of course, because man himself is part of the same overall reality, so that there is a fundamental affinity between the structures of his consciousness and the structures of the empirical world. Projection and reflection are movements within the same encompassing reality.

The same may be true of the projections of man's religious imagination. In any case it would seem that any theological method worthy of the name should be based on this possibility. This most emphatically does *not* mean a search for religious phenomena that will somehow manifest themselves as different from human projections. Nothing is immune to the relativization of socio-historical analysis. Whatever else these phenomena may be, they will *also* be human projections, products of human history, social constructions undertaken by human beings. The meta-empirical cannot be conceived of as a kind of enclave within the empirical world, any more, incidentally, than freedom can be conceived of as a hole in the fabric of causality. The theological decision will have to be that, "in, with, and under" the immense array of human projections, there are indicators of a reality that is truly "other" and that the religious imagination of man ultimately reflects.

These considerations also indicate a possible theological starting point, hardly an exclusive one, but one peculiarly apt to meet the challenge previously outlined. This is the starting point of anthropology, using the term in the continental sense, as referring to the philosophical enterprise that concerns itself with the question "What is man?" If the religious projections of man correspond to a reality that is superhuman and supernatural, then it seems logical to look for traces of this reality in the projector himself. This is not to suggest an empirical theology—that would be logically impossible—but rather a theology of very high empirical sensitivity that seeks to correlate its propositions with what can be empirically known. To the extent that its starting point is anthropological, such a theology will return to some of the fundamental concerns of Protestant liberalism—without, it is to be hoped, the latter's deference to the "cultured despisers of religion" and their assorted utopianisms.

3 Theological Possibilities: Starting with Man

If anthropology is understood here in a very broad sense, as any systematic inquiry into the constitution and condition of man, it will be clear that any kind of theology will have to include an anthropological dimension. After all, theological propositions only very rarely deal with the divine in and of itself, but rather in its relations to and significance for man. Even the most abstract speculations concerning the nature of the Trinity were much more salvation-oriented than theoretical in their underlying impetus, that is, they derived not from disinterested curiosity but from a burning concern for the redemption of man. The real question, then, is not so much whether theology relates to anthropology—it can hardly help doing so—but what kind of relation there will be.

Classical Protestant liberalism in the nineteenth century and up to about World War I was concerned with anthropology because, in one way or another, it sought to derive the truth of the Christian tradition from the data of human history. In line with the mood of this era of a triumphant bourgeois civilization, its anthropology was marked by a profound confidence in the rationality and perfectibility of man as well as by faith in the progressive course of man's history. Not surprisingly, this optimistic stance lost plausibility as the crisis of bourgeois civilization deepened in the wake of World War I. The naïve and situation-bound aspects of the liberal anthropology (in its religious as well as secular forms) became all too apparent. To the extent that neo-orthodox theology uncovered the shallow and utopian sides of liberalism, its protest was undoubtedly justified and even necessary. This, however, does not validate its own anthropological orientation.[27]

One of the key characteristics of the neo-orthodox reaction to theological liberalism was its violent rejection of the latter's historical and anthropological starting points. Liberalism had emphasized man's ways toward God, neo-orthodoxy emphasized God's dealings with man. No human experience was any longer to serve as the starting point of the theological enterprise, but rather the stark majesty of God's revelation that confronted man as negation, judgment, and grace. Neo-orthodoxy dared to pronounce once more a *Deus dixit*—"Thus saith the Lord."

In a very real sense neo-orthodoxy, in its original impulse, was anti-anthropological. There were to be no approaches from men to God, only the one approach from God to man, by means of a divine revelation that was due wholly to God's activity and not in any way rooted in man's nature or condition. Any anthropological statements (such as statements about man's sinfulness) could be made only in terms of this revelation. In other words, an anthropology could be theologically deduced, but there were no inductive possibilities *from* anthropology *to* theology. This orientation was, of course, sharpest in the early work of Karl Barth with its radical return to the God-centered and revelation-based thought of the Protestant Reformation. It is in this context that one can understand Barth's view that the decisive dividing line between Protestantism and Catholicism is the attitude toward the notion of *analogia entis* (the scholastic conception of an "analogy of being" between God and man)—Protestantism, according to Barth, had to pronounce a resounding "no!" to this notion.

The starkness of this position was too much even for many within the neo-orthodox movement. In the 1930s it was another Swiss theologian, Emil Brunner, in his controversy with Barth, who most clearly represented the modification of the neo-orthodox aversion to anthropological considerations. Significantly, Brunner was greatly interested in what he called the problem of the *Anknüpfungspunkt*—the "point of contact" between God's revelation and the human situation. This interest, largely fostered by practical considerations of evangelism and pastoral care, reintroduced anthropological perspectives into the neo-orthodox position. But now, quite logically, the anthropological propositions picked up by theologians tended to be those that stressed the "lostness" and misery of the human condition. The worse the picture of man, the greater the chance to make credible (*anknüpfen*) the claims of revelation. The gloomy anthropology of existentialism was amply suited to this purpose.

Later, particularly in America, the more pessimistic versions of Freudian anthropology were added. Thus concepts such as despair, *Angst*, "thrown-ness" became stock-in-trade terms of neo-orthodox theologians. For a while it seemed that the necessary counterpoint of the Christian proclamation was an anthropology of desperation—man, the object of the proclamation, was a murderous, incestuous figure, sunk in utter misery, without any hope except the hope of grace offered by God's revelation.

Needless to say, such an anthropology had a good deal to recommend itself during the twelve apocalyptic years between 1933 and 1945, and for some years after that. But even then there were some who were uneasy about the one-sidedness and even some who, with Albert Camus, came to feel that "in a time of pestilence" we learn "that there are more things to admire in men than to despise."[28]

The celebration of secularity that came to the fore in the theology of more recent years, of which John Robinson's *Honest to God* (1963) and Harvey Cox's *The Secular City* (1965) were popular high points, naturally turned to more cheerful anthropological perspectives. The moral mood came closer to an endorsement of "enjoy, enjoy!" than to the earlier recommendation to be as anxious as possible. The social world was once more seen as an arena of purposeful action for human betterment rather than as a quagmire of futilities. And this, again, had strong roots in the general intellectual trends of the time. After all, even Jean-Paul Sartre turned from his fascination with the alleged impossibility of love to a commitment to world-transforming revolutionary action. Such an optimistic reversal would appear to be a necessary condition for the secularization of Christianity. The secularizing theologian wishes to translate the tradition into terms that are immanent to "this eon." If such an undertaking is to have minimal attractiveness, "this eon" had better be worth the effort. Logically enough, notions such as "autonomy," "man come of age," and even "democratic humanism" came to be substituted for the earlier expressions of existential anguish. Indeed, if one looks at all this with a little detachment, one is strongly reminded of the children's game of rapidly changing grimaces—"now I'm crying"/"now I'm laughing"—only children don't construct a philosophy to go with each phase of the game.

Enough has been said earlier to indicate that, captive though we all are of the circumstances in which our thinking must take place, what is being suggested here is at least a measure of emancipation from this sequence of "mood theologies." The suggestion that theological thought revert to an anthropological starting point is motivated by the belief that such an anchorage in fundamental human experience might offer some protection against the constantly changing winds of cultural moods. In other words, I am not proposing a "more relevant" program or a new dating of our intellectual situation ("post-X" or "neo-Y"). Instead, I venture to hope that there may be theological possibilities whose life span is at least a little longer than the duration of any one cultural or socio-political crisis of the times.

What could an anthropological starting point mean for theology?

I am not in a position to answer this question by systematically confronting the vast literature that has accumulated in philosophical anthropology in recent decades. Nor can I present the design for a theological system that might emerge from this starting point. Such achievements must be left to professional philosophers and professional theologians (or perhaps, who knows, to teams that combine both types of expertise). But it is very unsatisfactory simply to produce assignments for other people. Very modestly then and with full awareness of my all too obvious limitations, let me give a few indications of the direction in which I think it is possible to move.

I would suggest that theological thought seek out what might be called *signals of transcendence* within the empirically given human situation. And I would further suggest that there are *prototypical human gestures* that may constitute such signals. What does this mean?

By signals of transcendence I mean phenomena that are to be found within the domain of our "natural" reality but that appear to point beyond that reality. In other words, I am not using transcendence here in a technical philosophical sense but literally, as the transcending of the normal, everyday world that I earlier identified with the notion of the "supernatural." By prototypical human gestures I mean certain reiterated acts and experiences that appear to express essential aspects of man's being, of the human animal as such. I do *not* mean what Jung called "archetypes"—potent symbols buried deep in the unconscious mind that are common to all men. The phenomena I am discussing are not "unconscious" and do not have to be excavated from the "depths" of the mind; they belong to ordinary everyday awareness.

One fundamental human trait, which is of crucial importance in understanding man's religious enterprise, is his propensity for order.[29] As the philosopher of history Eric Voegelin points out at the beginning of *Order and History*, his analysis of the various human conceptions of order: "The order of history emerges from the history of order. Every society is burdened with the task, under its concrete conditions, of creating an order that will endow the fact of its existence with meaning in terms of ends divine and human."[30] Any historical society is an order, a protective structure of meaning, erected in the face of chaos. Within this order the life of the group as well as the life of the individual makes sense. Deprived of such order, both group and individual are threatened with the most fundamental terror, the terror of chaos that Emile Durkheim called *anomie* (literally, a state of being "order-less").

Throughout most of human history men have believed that the created order of society, in one way or another, corresponds to an underlying order of the universe, a divine order that supports and justifies all human attempts at ordering. Now, clearly, not every such belief in correspondence can be true, and a philosophy of history may, like Voegelin's, be an inquiry into the relationship of true order to the different human attempts at ordering. But there is a more basic element to be considered, over and above the justification of this or that historically produced order. This is the human faith in order as such, a faith closely related to man's fundamental trust in reality. This faith is experienced not only in the history of societies and civilizations, but in the life of each individual—indeed, child psychologists tell us there can be no maturation without the presence of this faith at the outset of the socialization process. Man's propensity for order is grounded in a faith or trust that, ultimately, reality is "in order," "all right," "as it should be." Needless to say, there is no empirical method by which this faith can be tested. To assert it is itself an act of faith. But it is possible to proceed from the faith that is rooted in experience to the act of faith that transcends the empirical sphere, a procedure that could be called the *argument from ordering*.

In this fundamental sense, every ordering gesture is a signal of transcendence. This is certainly the case with the great ordering gestures that the historian of religion Mircea Eliade called "nomizations"—such as the archaic ceremonies in which a certain territory was solemnly incorporated into a society, or the celebration, in our own culture as in older ones, of the setting up of a new household through the marriage of two individuals. But it is equally true of more everyday occurrences. Consider the most ordinary, and probably most fundamental, of all—the ordering gesture by which a mother reassures her anxious child.

A child wakes up in the night, perhaps from a bad dream, and finds himself surrounded by darkness, alone, beset by nameless threats. At such a moment the contours of trusted reality are blurred or invisible, and in the terror of incipient chaos the child cries out for his mother. It is hardly an exaggeration to say that, at this moment, the mother is being invoked as a high priestess of protective order. It is she (and, in many cases, she alone) who has the power to banish the chaos and to restore the benign shape of the world. And, of course, any good mother will do just that. She will take the child and cradle him in the timeless gesture of the Magna Mater who became our Madonna. She will turn on a lamp, perhaps, which will encircle the scene with a warm glow of reassuring light. She will speak or sing to the child, and the content of this communication will invariably be the same—

"Don't be afraid—everything is in order, everything is all right." If all goes well, the child will be reassured, his trust in reality recovered, and in this trust he will return to sleep.

All this, of course, belongs to the most routine experiences of life and does not depend upon any religious preconceptions. Yet this common scene raises a far from ordinary question, which immediately introduces a religious dimension: *Is the mother lying to the child?* The answer, in the most profound sense, can be "no" only if there is some truth in the religious interpretation of human existence. Conversely, if the "natural" is the only reality there is, the mother is lying to the child—lying out of love, to be sure, and obviously *not* lying to the extent that her reassurance is grounded in the fact of this love—but, in the final analysis, lying all the same. Why? *Because the reassurance, transcending the immediately present two individuals and their situation, implies a statement about reality as such.*

To become a parent is to take on the role of world-builder and world-protector. This is so, of course, in the obvious sense that parents provide the environment in which a child's socialization takes place and serve as mediators to the child of the entire world of the particular society in question. But it is also so in a less obvious, more profound sense, which is brought out in the scene just described. The role that a parent takes on represents not only the order of this or that society, but order as such, the underlying order of the universe that it makes sense to trust. It is this role that may be called the role of high priestess. It is a role that the mother in this scene plays willy-nilly, regardless of her own awareness or (more likely) lack of awareness of just what it is she is representing. "*Everything* is in order, *everything* is all right"—this is the basic formula of maternal and parental reassurance. Not just this particular anxiety, not just this particular pain—but *everything* is all right. The formula can, without in any way violating it, be translated into a statement of cosmic scope—"Have trust in being." This is precisely what the formula intrinsically implies. And if we are to believe the child psychologists (which we have good reason to do in this instance), this is an experience that is absolutely essential to the process of becoming a human person. Put differently, at the very center of the process of becoming fully human, at the core of *humanitas*, we find an experience of trust in the order of reality. Is this experience an illusion? Is the individual who represents it a liar?

If reality is coextensive with the "natural" reality that our empirical reason can grasp, then the experience *is* an illusion and the role that embodies it *is* a lie. For then it is perfectly obvious that everything is *not* in order, is *not* all right. The world that the child is being told to trust is the same world in which he will eventually die. If there is no other world, then the ultimate truth about this one is that eventually it will kill the child as it will kill his mother. This would not, to be sure, detract from the real presence of love and its very real comforts; it would even give this love a quality of tragic heroism. Nevertheless, the final truth would be not love but terror, not light but darkness. The nightmare of chaos, not the transitory safety of order, would be the final reality of the human situation. For, in the end, we must all find ourselves in darkness, alone with the night that will swallow us up. The face of reassuring love, bending over our terror, will then be nothing except an image of merciful illusion. In that case the last word about religion is Freud's. Religion is the childish fantasy that our parents run the universe for our benefit, a fantasy from which the mature individual must free himself in order to attain whatever measure of stoic resignation he is capable of.

It goes without saying that the preceding argument is not a moral one. It does not condemn the mother for this charade of world-building, if it be a charade. It does not dispute the right of atheists to be parents (though it is not without interest that there have been atheists who have rejected parenthood for exactly these reasons). The argument from ordering is metaphysical rather than ethical. To restate it: In the observable human propensity to order reality there is an intrinsic impulse to give cosmic scope to this order, an impulse that implies not only that human order in some way corresponds to an order that transcends it, but that this transcendent order is of such a character that man can trust himself and his destiny to it. There is a variety of human roles that represent this conception of order, but the most fundamental is the parental role. Every parent (or, at any rate, every parent who loves his child) takes upon himself the representation of a universe that is ultimately in order and ultimately trustworthy. This representation can be justified only within a religious (strictly speaking a supernatural) frame of reference. In this frame of reference the natural world within which we are born, love, and die is not the only world, but only the foreground of another world in which love is not annihilated in death, and in which, therefore, the trust in the power of love to banish chaos is justified. Thus man's ordering propensity implies a transcendent order, and each ordering gesture is a signal of this transcendence. The parental role is not based on a loving lie. On the contrary, it is a witness to the ultimate truth of man's situation in reality. In that case, it is perfectly possible (even, if one is so inclined, in Freudian terms) to analyze religion as a cosmic projection of the child's experience of the protective order of parental love. What is projected is, however, itself a reflection, an imitation, of ultimate reality. Religion, then, is not only (from the point of view of empirical reason) a projection of human order, but (from the point of view of what might be called *inductive faith*) the ultimately true vindication of human order.

Since the term "inductive faith" will appear a number of times, its meaning should be clarified. I use induction to mean any process of thought that begins with experience. Deduction is the reverse process; it begins with ideas that precede experience. By "inductive faith," then, I mean a religious process of thought that begins with facts of human experience; conversely, "deductive faith" begins with certain assumptions (notably assumptions about divine revelation) that cannot be tested by experience. Put simply, inductive faith moves from human experience to statements about God, deductive faith from statements about God to interpretations of human experience.

Closely related to, though still distinct from, the foregoing considerations is what I will call the *argument from play*. Once more, as the Dutch historian Johan Huizinga has shown, we are dealing with a basic experience of man.[31] Ludic, or playful, elements can be found in just about any sector of human culture, to the point where it can be argued that culture as such would be impossible without this dimension. One aspect of play that Huizinga analyzes in some detail is the fact that play sets up a separate universe of discourse, with its own rules, which suspends, "for the duration," the rules and general assumptions of the "serious" world. One of the most important assumptions thus suspended is the time structure of ordinary social life. When one is playing, one is on a different time, no longer measured by the standard units of the larger society, but rather by the peculiar ones of the game in question. In the "serious" world it may be 11 A.M., on such and such a day, month, and year. But in the universe in which one is playing it may be the third round, the fourth act, the *allegro* movement, or the second kiss. In playing, one steps out of one time into another.[32]

This is true of all play. Play always constructs an enclave within the "serious" world of everyday social life, and an enclave within the latter's chronology as well. This is also true of play that creates pain rather than joy. It may be 11 A.M., say, but in the universe of the torturer it will be thumbscrews time again. Nevertheless one of the most pervasive features of play is that it is usually a joyful activity. Indeed, when it ceases to be joyful and becomes misery or even indifferent routine, we tend to think of this as a perversion of its intrinsic character. Joy is play's intention. When this intention is actually realized, in joyful play, the time structure of the playful universe takes on a very specific quality—namely, *it becomes eternity.* This is probably true of all experiences of intense joy, even when they are not enveloped in the separate reality of play. This is the final insight of Nietzsche's Zarathustra in the midnight song: "All joy wills eternity—wills deep, deep eternity!"[33] This intention is, however, particularly patent in the joy experienced in play, precisely because the playful universe has a temporal dimension that is more than momentary and that can be perceived as a distinct structure. In other words, in joyful play it appears as if one were stepping not only from one chronology into another, but from time into eternity. Even as one remains conscious of the poignant reality of that other, "serious" time in which one is moving toward death, one apprehends joy as being, in some barely conceivable way, a joy forever. Joyful play appears to suspend, or bracket, the reality of our "living towards death" (as Heidegger aptly described our "serious" condition).

It is this curious quality, which belongs to all joyful play, that explains the liberation and peace such play provides. In early childhood, of course, the suspension is unconscious, since there is as yet no consciousness of death. In later life play brings about a beatific reiteration of childhood. When adults play with genuine joy, they momentarily regain the deathlessness of childhood. This becomes most apparent when such play occurs in the actual face of acute suffering and dying. It is this that stirs us about men making music in a city under bombardment or a man doing mathematics on his deathbed. C. S. Lewis, in a sermon preached at the beginning of World War II, put this eloquently: "Human life has always been lived on the edge of a precipice. . . . Men . . . propound mathematical theorems in beleaguered cities, conduct metaphysical arguments in condemned cells, make jokes on scaffolds, discuss the last new poem while advancing to the walls of Quebec, and comb their hair at Thermopylae. This is not *panache*: it is our nature."[34] It is our nature because, as Huizinga suggests, man is profoundly *homo ludens*. It is his ludic constitution that allows man, even at Thermopylae, to regain and ec-statically realize the deathless joy of his childhood.

Some little girls are playing hopscotch in the park. They are completely intent on their game, closed to the world outside it, happy in their concentration. Time has stood still for them—or, more accurately, it has been collapsed into the movements of the game. The outside world has, for the duration of the game, ceased to exist. And, by implication (since the little girls may not be very conscious of this), pain and death, which are the law of that world, have also ceased to exist. Even the adult observer of this scene, who is perhaps all too conscious of pain and death, is momentarily drawn into the beatific immunity.

In the playing of adults, at least on certain occasions, the suspension of time and of the "serious" world in which people suffer and die becomes explicit. Just before the Soviet troops occupied Vienna in 1945, the Vienna Philharmonic gave one of its scheduled concerts. There was fighting in the immediate proximity of the city, and the concertgoers could hear the rumbling of the guns in the distance. The entry of the Soviet army interrupted the concert schedule—if I'm not mistaken, for about a week. Then the concerts resumed, as scheduled. In the universe of this particular play, the world-shattering events of the Soviet invasion, the overthrow of one empire and the cataclysmic appearance of another, meant a small interruption in the program. Was this simply a case of callousness, of indifference to suffering? Perhaps in the case of some individuals, but, basically, I would say not. It was rather an affirmation of the ultimate triumph of all human gestures of creative beauty over the gestures of destruction, and even over the ugliness of war and death.

The logic of the argument from play is very similar to that of the argument from order. The experience of joyful play is not something that must be sought on some mystical margin of existence. It can be readily found in the reality of ordinary life. Yet within this experienced reality it constitutes a signal of transcendence, because its intrinsic intention points beyond itself and beyond man's "nature" to a "supernatural" justification. Again, it will be perfectly clear that this justification cannot be empirically proved. Indeed, the experience can be plausibly interpreted as a merciful illusion, a regression to childish magic (along the lines, say, of the Freudian theory of wishful fantasy). The religious justification of the experience can be achieved only in an act of faith. The point, however, is that this faith is inductive— it does not rest on a mysterious revelation, but rather on what we experience in our common, ordinary lives. All men have experienced the deathlessness of childhood and we may assume that, even if only once or twice, all men have experienced transcendent joy in adulthood. Under the aspect of inductive faith, religion is the final vindication of childhood and of joy, and of all gestures that replicate these.

Another essential element of the human situation is hope, and there is an *argument from hope* within the same logic of inductive faith. In recent philosophical anthropology, this element has been particularly emphasized by the French philosopher Gabriel Marcel (in the context of a Christian existentialism) and by the German philosopher Ernst Bloch (in a Marxist context). A number of theologians, influenced by Bloch, have taken up this theme in their dialogue with Marxism.[35]

Bloch emphasizes that man's being cannot be adequately understood except in connection with man's unconquerable propensity to hope for the future. As a Marxist, Bloch, of course, relates this to the revolutionary hope of transforming the world for human betterment. Some theologians have argued that such hope is also the essence of Christianity (and, incidentally, that therefore Christians should not necessarily be anti-revolutionary). This is not the place to discuss these developments, though it should be said that the argument here is compatible with but not directly indebted to them.[36]

Human existence is always oriented toward the future. Man

exists by constantly extending his being into the future, both in his consciousness and in his activity. Put differently, man realizes himself in projects. An essential dimension of this "futurity" of man is hope. It is through hope that men overcome the difficulties of any given here and now. And it is through hope that men find meaning in the face of extreme suffering. A key ingredient of most (but not all) theodicies is hope. The specific content of such hope varies. In earlier periods of human history, when the concept of the individual and his unique worth was not as yet so sharply defined, this hope was commonly invested in the future of the group. The individual might suffer and die, be defeated in his most important projects, but the group (clan, or tribe, or people) would live on and eventually triumph. Often, of course, theodicies were based on the hope of an individual afterlife, in which the sufferings of this earthly life would be vindicated and left behind. Through most of human history, both collective and individual theodicies of hope were legitimated in religious terms. Under the impact of secularization, ideologies of this-worldly hope have come to the fore as theodicies (the Marxist one being the most important of late). In any case, human hope has always asserted itself most intensely in the face of experiences that seemed to spell utter defeat, most intensely of all in the face of the final defeat of death. Thus the profoundest manifestations of hope are to be found in gestures of courage undertaken in defiance of death.

Courage, of course, can be exhibited by individuals committed to every kind of cause—good, bad, or indifferent. A cause is not justified by the courage of its proponents. After all, there were some very courageous Nazis. The kind of courage I am interested in here is linked to hopes for human creation, justice, or compassion; that is, linked to other gestures of *humanitas*— the artist who, against all odds and even in failing health, strives to finish his creative act; the man who risks his life to defend or save innocent victims of oppression; the man who sacrifices his own interests and comfort to come to the aid of afflicted fellow men. There is no need to belabor the point with examples. Suffice it to say that it is this kind of courage and hope that I have in mind in this argument.

We confront here once more, then, observable phenomena of the human situation whose intrinsic intention appears to be a depreciation or even denial of the reality of death. Once more, under the aspect of inductive faith, these phenomena are signals of transcendence, pointers toward a religious interpretation of the human situation. Psychologists tell us (correctly no doubt) that, though we may fear our own death, we cannot really imagine it. Our innermost being shrinks from the image and even theoretical detachment seems to be caught in this fundamental incapacity. It is partly on this basis that Sartre has criticized Heidegger's concept of "living unto death," arguing that we are fundamentally incapable of such an attitude. The only death we can experience, Sartre maintains, is the death of others; our own death can never be part of our experience, and it eludes even our imagination. Yet it is precisely in the face of the death of others, and especially of others that we love, that our rejection of death asserts itself most loudly. It is here, above all, that everything we are calls out for a hope that will refute the empirical fact. It would seem, then, that both psychologically (in the failure to imagine his own death) and morally (in his violent denial of the death of others) a "no!" to death is profoundly rooted in the very being of man.

This refusal is to be found in more than what Karl Jaspers called the "marginal situations" of human life—such extreme experiences as critical illness, war, or other natural or social catastrophes. There are, of course, trivial expressions of hope that do not contain this dimension—"I hope that we will have good weather for our picnic." But any hope that, in whatever way, involves the individual as a whole already implicitly contains this ultimate refusal—"I hope to finish my work as a scientist as well as I can"—"I hope to make a success of my marriage"—"I hope to be brave when I must speak up against the majority." All these contain an ultimate refusal to capitulate before the inevitability of death. After all, even as I express these limited hopes, I know that I may die before my work is finished, that the woman I marry may even now be afflicted by a fatal disease, or that some majorities, if outraged enough, may kill me. The denial of death implicit in hope becomes more manifest, of course, in the extreme cases—"I hope to finish my work as well as I can, despite the war that is about to destroy my city" —"I shall marry this woman, despite what the doctor has just told me about her condition"—"I shall say my piece, despite the murderous plans of my enemies."

It is again very clear that both the psychological and moral aspects of such denial can be explained within the confines of empirical reason. Our fear of death is instinctually rooted and presumably has a biological survival value in the process of evolution. The psychological paralysis before the thought of our own death can be plausibly explained in terms of the combination of the instinctual recoil before death and the peculiarly human knowledge of its inevitability. The moral refusal to accept the death of others can equally plausibly be explained as nothing but a "rationalization" (in the Freudian sense) of instinctual and psychological forces. In this perspective, the denial of death and any manifestation of hope (religious or otherwise) that embodies this denial is a symptom of "childishness." This, indeed, was the burden of Freud's analysis of religion. Against such "childish" hopes there stands the "mature" acceptance of what is taken to be final reality, an essentially stoic attitude which, in the case of Freud, Philip Rieff has aptly called the "ethic of honesty."[37] It hardly needs to be said that this kind of stoicism merits the deepest respect and, in fact, constitutes one of the most impressive attitudes of which man is capable. Freud's calm courage in the face of Nazi barbarity and in his own final illness may be cited as a prime example of this human achievement.

Nevertheless the twin concepts of "childishness" and "maturity" are based on an a priori metaphysical choice that does not follow of necessity from the facts of the matter. The choice does not even necessarily follow if we are convinced (which, let it be added, I am not) by the Freudian interpretation of the psychological genesis of death-denying hope. Man's "no!" to death—be it in the frantic fear of his own annihilation, in moral outrage at the death of a loved other, or in death-defying acts of courage and self-sacrifice—appears to be an intrinsic constituent of his being. There seems to be a death-refusing hope at the very core of our *humanitas*. While empirical reason indicates that this hope is an illusion, there is something in us that, however shamefacedly in an age of triumphant rationality, goes on saying "no!" and even says "no!" to the ever so plausible explanations of empirical reason.

In a world where man is surrounded by death on all sides, he continues to be a being who says "no!" to death—and through this "no!" is brought to faith in another world, the reality of which would validate his hope as something other than illusion. It is tempting to think here of a kind of Cartesian reduction, in which one finally arrives at a root fact of consciousness that says "no!" to death and "yes!" to hope. In any case, the argument from hope follows the logical direction of induction from what is empirically given. It starts from experience but takes seriously those implications or intentions within experience that transcend it—and takes them, once again, as signals of a transcendent reality.

Inductive faith acknowledges the omnipresence of death (and thus of the futility of hope) in "nature," but it also takes into account the intentions within our "natural" experience of hope that point toward a "supernatural" fulfillment. This reinterpretation of our experience encompasses rather than contradicts the various explanations of empirical reason (be they psychological, sociological, or what-have-you). Religion, in justifying this reinterpretation, is the ultimate vindication of hope and courage, just as it is the ultimate vindication of childhood and joy. By the same token, religion vindicates the gestures in which hope and courage are embodied in human action—including, given certain conditions, the gestures of revolutionary hope and, in the ultimate irony of redemption, the courage of stoic resignation.

A somewhat different sort of reasoning is involved in what I will call the *argument from damnation*. This refers to experiences in which our sense of what is humanly permissible is so fundamentally outraged that the only adequate response to the offense as well as to the offender seems to be a curse of supernatural dimensions. I advisedly choose this negative form of reasoning, as against what may at first appear to be a more obvious argument from a positive sense of justice. The latter argument would, of course, lead into the territory of "natural law" theories, where I am reluctant to go at this point. As is well known, these theories have been particularly challenged by the relativizing insights of both the historian and the social scientist, and while I suspect that these challenges can be met, this is not the place to negotiate the question. The negative form of the argument makes the intrinsic intention of the human sense of justice stand out much more sharply as a signal of transcendence over and beyond sociohistorical relativities.

The ethical and legal discussion that surrounded, and still surrounds, the trials of Nazi war criminals has given every thinking person, at least in Western countries, an unhappy opportunity to reflect upon these matters. I will not discuss here either the agonizing question "How can such things have been done by human beings?" or the practical question of how the institution of the law is to deal with evil of this scope. In America both questions have been debated very fruitfully in the wake of the publication of Hannah Arendt's *Eichmann in Jerusalem*, and I do not wish to contribute to the debate here. What concerns me at the moment is not how Eichmann is to be explained or how Eichmann should have been dealt with, but rather *the character and intention of our condemnation* of Eichmann. For here is a case (as Arendt revealed, especially in the last pages of her book) in which condemnation can be posited as an absolute and compelling necessity, irrespective of how the case is explained or of what practical consequences one may wish to draw from it. Indeed, a refusal to condemn in absolute terms would appear to offer prima facie evidence not only of a profound failure in the understanding of justice, but more profoundly of a fatal impairment of *humanitas*.

There are certain deeds that cry out to heaven. These deeds are not only an outrage to our moral sense, they seem to violate a fundamental awareness of the constitution of our humanity. In this way, these deeds are not only evil, but *monstrously evil*. And it is this monstrosity that seems to compel even people normally or professionally given to such perspectives to suspend relativizations. It is one thing to say that moralities are socio-historical products, which are relative in time and space. It is quite another thing to say that *therefore* the deeds of an Eichmann can be viewed with scientific detachment as simply an instance of one such morality—and thus, ultimately, can be considered a matter of taste. Of course, it is possible, and for certain purposes may be very useful, to attempt a dispassionate analysis of the case, but it seems impossible to let the matter rest there. It also seems impossible to say something like, "Well, we may not like this at all, we may be outraged or appalled, but that is only because we come from a certain background and have been socialized into certain values—we would react quite differently if we had been socialized [or, for that matter, resocialized, as Eichmann presumably was] in a different way." To be sure, *within a scientific frame of reference*, such a statement may be quite admissible. The crucial point, though, is that this whole relativizing frame of reference appears woefully inadequate to the phenomenon if it is taken as the last word on the matter. Not only are we constrained to condemn, and to condemn absolutely, but, if we should be in a position to do so, we would feel constrained to take action on the basis of this certainty. The imperative to save a child from murder, even at the cost of killing the putative murderer, appears to be curiously immune to relativizing analysis. It seems impossible to deny it even when, because of cowardice or calculation, it is not obeyed.

The signal of transcendence is to be found in a clarification of this "impossibility." Clearly, the murder of children is both practically and theoretically "possible." It can be done, and has been done in innumerable massacres of the innocent stretching back to the dawn of history. It can also be justified by those who do it, however abhorrent their justifications may seem to others. And it can be explained in a variety of ways by an outside observer. None of these "possibilities," however, touch upon the fundamental "impossibility" that, when everything that can be said about it has been said, still impresses us as the fundamental truth. The transcendent element manifests itself in two steps. First, our condemnation is absolute and certain. It does not permit modification or doubt, and it is made in the conviction that it applies to all times and to all men as well as to the perpetrator or putative perpetrator of the particular deed. In other words, we give the condemnation the status of a necessary and universal truth. But, as sociological analysis shows more clearly than any other, this truth, while empirically given in our situation as men, cannot be empirically demonstrated to be either necessary or universal. We are, then, faced with a quite simple alternative: Either we deny that there is here anything that can be called truth—a choice that would make us deny what we experience most profoundly as our own being; or we must look beyond the realm of our "natural" experience for a validation of our certainty. Second, the condemnation does not seem to exhaust its intrinsic intention in terms of this world alone. Deeds that cry out to heaven also cry out for hell. This is the point that was brought out very clearly in the debate over Eichmann's execution. Without going into the question of either the legality or the wisdom of the execution, it is safe to say that there was a very general feeling that "hanging is not enough" in this case. But what would have been "enough"? If Eichmann, instead of being hanged, had been tortured to death in the most lengthy and cruel manner imaginable, would this have been "enough"? A negative answer seems inevitable. No human punishment is "enough" in the case of deeds as monstrous as these. These are deeds that demand not only condemnation, but *damnation* in the full religious meaning of the word—that is, the doer not only puts himself outside the community of men; he also separates himself in a final way from a moral order that transcends the human community, and thus invokes a retribution that is more than human.

Just as certain gestures can be interpreted as anticipations of redemption, so other gestures can be viewed as anticipations of hell (hell here meaning no more or less than the state of being damned, both here and now and also beyond the confines of this life and this world). We have interpreted the prototypical gesture of a mother holding her child in protective reassurance as a signal of transcendence. A few years ago, a picture was printed that contains the prototypical countergesture. It was taken somewhere in eastern Europe during World War II at a mass execution—of Jews, or of Russians or Poles, nobody seems to know for sure. The picture shows a woman holding a child, supporting it with one hand and with the other pressing its face into her shoulder, and a few feet away a German soldier with raised rifle, taking aim. More recently two pictures have come out of the war in Vietnam that, as it were, separate the components of this paradigm of hell (and, when taken together, serve to remind us that damnation very rarely follows the political dividing lines drawn by men). One picture, taken at an interrogation of "Vietcong suspects,'' shows an American soldier holding a rifle against the head of a woman of indeterminate age, her face lined with anguish. Whether or not the rifle was eventually fired, the possibility is implied in the threatening gesture. The other picture was taken during the Tet offensive of the Vietcong in early 1968, in a military billet in Saigon where the Vietcong had massacred the families of officers of the South Vietnamese army. It shows an officer carrying his dead daughter in his arms. The lines on his face are like those on the face of the woman being interrogated. Only here we do not see the man with the rifle.

I would argue that both gesture and countergesture imply transcendence, albeit in opposite ways. Both may be understood, under the aspect of inductive faith, as pointing to an ultimate, religious context in human experience. Just as religion vindicates the gesture of protective reassurance, even when it is performed in the face of death, so it also vindicates the ultimate condemnation of the countergesture of inhumanity, precisely because religion provides a context for damnation. Hope and damnation are two aspects of the same, encompassing vindication. The duality, I am inclined to think, is important. To be sure, religious hope offers a theodicy and therefore consolation to the victims of inhumanity. But it is equally significant that religion provides damnation for the perpetrators of inhumanity. The massacre of the innocent (and, in a terrible way, all of history can be seen as this) raises the question of the justice and power of God. It also, however, suggests the necessity of hell—not so much as a confirmation of God's justice, but rather as a vindication of our own.

Finally, there is an *argument from humor*.[38] A good deal has been written about the phenomenon of humor, much of it in a very humorless vein. In recent thought, the two most influential theories on the subject have probably been those of Freud and Bergson.[39] Both interpret humor as the apprehension of a fundamental discrepancy—in Freud's theory, the discrepancy between the demands of superego and libido; in Bergson's, between a living organism and the mechanical world. I have strong reservations about either theory, but I readily concede one common proposition—that the comic (which is the object of any humorous perception) is fundamentally discrepancy, incongruity, incommensurability. This leads to a question, which Freud does not raise because of his psychological perspective and which Bergson, I think, answers incorrectly, as to the nature of the two realities that are discrepant or incongruous with respect to each other.

I agree with Bergson's description: "A situation is invariably comic when it belongs simultaneously to two altogether independent series of events and is capable of being interpreted in two entirely different meanings at the same time."[40] But I insist upon adding that this comic quality always refers to *human* situations, not to encounters between organisms and the nonorganic. The biological as such is not comic. Animals become comic only when we view them anthropomorphically, that is, when we imbue them with human characteristics. Within the human sphere, just about any discrepancy can strike us as funny. Discrepancy is the stuff of which jokes are made, and frequently it is the punch line that reveals the "entirely different meaning." The little Jew meets the big Negro. The mouse wants to sleep with the elephant. The great philosopher loses his pants. But I would go further than this and suggest that there is one fundamental discrepancy from which all other comic discrepancies are derived—the discrepancy between man and universe. It is *this* discrepancy that makes the comic an essentially human phenomenon and humor an intrinsically human trait. *The comic reflects the imprisonment of the human spirit in the world*. This is why, as has been pointed out over and over since classical antiquity, comedy and tragedy are at root closely related. Both are commentaries on man's finitude—if one wants to put it in existentialist terms, on his condition of "thrown-ness." If this is so, then the comic is an objective dimension of man's reality, not just a subjective or psychological reaction to that reality. One of the most moving testimonies to this is that made by the French writer David Rousset, commenting on his time spent in a Nazi concentration camp. He writes that one of the few lasting lessons he took with him from this period was the recognition that the comic was an objective fact that was *there* and could be perceived as such, no matter how great the inner terror and anguish of the mind perceiving it.

There is an additional point to be made. Humor not only recognizes the comic discrepancy in the human condition, it also relativizes it, and thereby suggests that the tragic perspective on the discrepancies of the human condition can also be relativized. At least for the duration of the comic perception, the tragedy of man is bracketed. By laughing at the imprisonment of the human spirit, humor implies that this imprisonment is not final but will be overcome, and by this implication provides yet another signal of transcendence—in this instance in the form of an intimation of redemption. I would thus argue that humor, like childhood and play, can be seen as an ultimately religious vindication of joy.

Humor mocks the "serious" business of this world and the mighty who carry it out. There is a story that when Tamerlane conquered Persia he ordered the poet Hafiz to be brought before him and confronted him with one of his poems, in which he had promised all the glories of Samarkand for the mole on his sweetheart's cheek. "How dare you offer the splendor of my imperial capital for the shoddy attractions of a Persian whore?" Tamerlane angrily demanded. "Your majesty, it is from you that I have learned the habits of generosity," Hafiz is said to have replied. According to the story, Tamerlane laughed and spared the poet's life. He might well have reacted differently, conquerors and empire-builders not usually being endowed with much appreciation for humor. But whatever the outcome of such encounters between tyrants and poets, the question I would always ask is this: Who, in the end, is to be pitied—the one who holds the world in his powerful hands, or the one who laughs at him? The "serious" answer is, of course, that power is not to be pitied, that the pitiful are always the victims of power. Humor, at least for the instant in which it perceives the comic dimensions of the situation, gives the opposite answer. The one to be finally pitied is the one who has an illusion. And power is the final illusion, while laughter reveals the final truth. To a degree, this can be said without any reference to transcendence. Empirical reason knows that all power is precarious and that eventually even Tamerlane must die. But the revelation of laughter points beyond these empirical facts. Power is ultimately an illusion because it cannot transcend the limits of the empirical world. Laughter can—and does every time it relativizes the seemingly rocklike necessities of this world.

A prototypical manifestation of the comic in Western literature is the figure of Don Quixote. And a prototypical embodiment of the gestures of humorous liberation is the clown. Both figures illustrate the basic alternatives in interpreting man's imprisonment in the world. In Cervantes' novel, the profoundly comic rebellion of Quixote against the imprisoning walls of the empirical world ends in tragic failure. At the end, in Alfred Schutz's words, Quixote is "a homecomer to a world to which he does not belong, enclosed in everyday reality as in a prison, and tortured by the most cruel jailer: the common-sense reason which is conscious of its own limits."[41] No other conclusion is possible from the point of view of empirical reason. Another conclusion, the specifically religious one, is eloquently expressed by Enid Welsford in the last paragraph of her history of the clown as a social and literary figure: "To those who do not repudiate the religious insight of the race, the human spirit is uneasy in this world because it is at home elsewhere, and escape from the prison house is possible not only in fancy but in fact. The theist believes in possible beatitude, because he disbelieves in the dignified isolation of humanity. To him, therefore, romantic comedy is serious literature because it is a foretaste of the truth: the Fool is wiser than the Humanist; and clownage is less frivolous than the deification of humanity."[42] In a religious frame of reference, it is Quixote's hope rather than Sancho Panza's "realism" that is ultimately vindicated, and the gestures of the clown have a sacramental dignity. Religion reinterprets the meaning of the comic and vindicates laughter.

This is by no means an exhaustive or exclusive list of human gestures that may be seen as signals of transcendence. To provide one would entail constructing a philosophical anthropology and, on top of that, a theological system to go with it. I am not prepared to be quite as Quixotic as that! But I do want to go at least a few steps beyond setting up a program and suggest how it might be possible to theologize from an anthropological starting point. My choice of examples may not be convincing to everyone and, in any case, is fairly arbitrary. I could have chosen other examples, though I would contend that the ones just discussed are particularly useful because they all refer to very basic human experiences. I have deliberately omitted any discussion of claims to direct religious experience (in the sense of experience of the supernatural). This is by no means intended to depreciate efforts to study and understand such phenomena; it merely follows from my earlier expressed belief that theological thought would do well to turn from the projections to the projector, and thus to empirical data about man. It is fairly clear that mysticism, or any other alleged experience of supernatural realities, is not accessible to everyone. Almost by definition, it partakes of the quality of the esoteric. My aim has been to explore theological possibilities that take as their starting point what is generally accessible to all men. I have therefore limited myself to a discussion of phenomena that can be found in everybody's ordinary life. Even the argument from damnation remains within the context of the "ordinary," in the sense that it does not presuppose any special illumination or intervention from beyond the human sphere. I make no claim for this method over any other, but, to repeat, it is a possible solution to the vertigo of relativity. It will appeal particularly, I think, to those who have passed through the "fiery brook" of sociological relativization.

It goes without saying that this procedure raises very complex philosophical questions. Again, I am not prepared to negotiate them here. But two disclaimers should be made right away. My procedure does *not* presuppose a static "human nature," somehow outside history. Neither does it presuppose a theory of historical "evolution" or "progress." There are some prototypical human gestures that appear timeless and that may be considered as constants in history. It may be that there are necessary and necessarily recurrent expressions of *humanitas*. But no one can deny that there have been far-reaching changes in the understanding of *humanitas* in the course of history. For example, our present understanding of the relationship between *humanitas* and slavery is anything but timeless. Nevertheless I maintain that our understanding has greater truth than, say, the understanding of classical antiquity. We may today be in the process of discovering new truths about the constitution and scope of *humanitas* in the area of human rights. I think that contemporary views on the equality of sexes (including the "third sex" of so-called "erotic minorities") and of the races, or on the "impossibility" of capital punishment, constitute genuinely new discoveries of truths about man. At the same time, it would almost certainly be an error to think of such truths as "evolving" naturally or inevitably in the course of history, or to think of history as a straight line of "progress," ascending of necessity to ever greater knowledge of the truth about man. Truths can be discovered or rediscovered. Truths can also be lost and forgotten again. History is not the night in which all cats are gray, but neither is it a giant escalator ascending to the point at which we happen to stand. Each claim to truth must be looked at on its own merits—in "immediacy to God," as the nineteenth-century historian Ranke would have it —and simultaneously in full awareness of its socio-historical location. Thus it is in no way certain, but altogether possible, that we know some things today about the scope of *humanitas* that have never been known before. It is also possible that there was a secret conclave of Aztec priests who knew something we have not even dreamed of—and that this truth perished with them, never to be recovered. A certain balance of brashness and modesty, in about equal measures, is a virtue when it comes to anthropological inquiry.

Let us return once more to the juxtaposition of the "natural" and the "supernatural," as these terms were used earlier. I maintain that there is a dichotomy in the human situation between a middle ground, which is the realm of ordinary, everyday life in society, and various marginal realms in which the taken-for-granted assumptions of the former realm are threatened or put in question. As Alfred Schutz has shown, the middle ground, which we take for granted as normality and sanity, can be maintained (that is, inhabited) only if we suspend all doubt about its validity. Without this suspension of doubt, everyday life would be impossible, if only because it would be constantly invaded by the "fundamental anxiety" caused by our knowledge and fear of death. This implies that all human societies and their institutions are, at their root, a barrier against naked terror.[43]

Nevertheless most historical societies have related the marginal experiences to those of the middle ground in a variety of ways, both practical and theoretical. There have been rituals to assuage, but at the same time to represent, the terror of the margins. Funeral rites or ceremonies regarding sexuality are examples of this. There have been theories that served to integrate the same margins with

83

what Schutz called the "paramount reality" of everyday life, but that in doing so took cognizance of the reality of marginal experience. In other words, most historical societies have remained open to the metaphysical. Human life has always had a day-side and a night-side, and, inevitably, because of the practical requirements of man's being in the world, it has always been the day-side that has received the strongest "accent of reality." But the night-side, even if exorcised, was rarely denied. One of the most astonishing consequences of secularization has been just this denial. Modern society has banished the night from consciousness, as far as this is possible. The treatment of death in modern society, especially in America, is the sharpest manifestation of this.[44] Much more generally, modern society has not only sealed up the old metaphysical questions in practice, but (especially in the Anglo-Saxon countries) has generated philosophical positions that deny the meaningfulness of these questions. "What is the purpose of my life?" "Why must I die?" "Where do I come from and where will I go?" "Who am I?" —all such questions are not only suppressed in practice, but are theoretically liquidated by relegating them to meaninglessness. To repeat a simile used before, the reality of a middle-aged businessman drowsily digesting his lunch is elevated to the status of final philosophical authority. All questions that do not correspond to this reality are ruled to be inadmissible. The denial of metaphysics may here be identified with the triumph of triviality.

How long such a shrinkage in the scope of human experience can remain plausible is debatable. In any case, it constitutes a profound impoverishment. Both in practice and in theoretical thought, human life gains the greatest part of its richness from the capacity for ecstasy, by which I do not mean the alleged experiences of the mystic, but any experience of stepping outside the taken-for-granted reality of everyday life, any openness to the mystery that surrounds us on all sides. A philosophical anthropology worthy of the name will have to regain a perception of these experiences, and with this regain a metaphysical dimension. The theological method suggested here as a possibility will contribute to this rediscovery of ecstasy and metaphysics as crucial dimensions of human life, and by the same token to the recovery of lost riches of both experience and thought.

4 Theological Possibilities: Confronting the Traditions

It should be amply clear by now that, however it may have appeared in some early sections of this book, I am *not* proposing a theological program of conservative restoration. My repudiation of the trivialities of recent "radical" theology, and of the secularized consciousness that this theology seeks to legitimate, is not an invitation to seek refuge in the firm (*sic*) fortresses of tradition. The terms I have used to outline a possible theological method—"anthropological starting point," "empirically given," and "inductive faith" —are intrinsically repulsive to most conservative forms of theology. Their natural affinity is with theological liberalism, especially that movement of Protestant liberal theology that began with Schleiermacher and, as I have suggested, was only temporarily interrupted by the neo-orthodox reaction following World War I.

Indeed, it is perhaps two different understandings of the *relationship* between faith and reason that constitute the crucial division between conservative and liberal modes of theologizing. It is most inaccurate to reproach all conservative theology with irrationality or all liberal theology with timidity of faith. The issue lies, rather, in the manner in which two movements of the mind are related. Conservative theology, however rational it may be in its method, tends to *deduce* from the tradition. Liberal theology, however much it may emphasize the necessity of faith, tends to *induce* from generally accessible experience. It would be puerile to make moral or psychological judgments on this difference. Let me simply emphasize once more my conviction that it is the method of "inductive faith" that holds the greatest promise of new approaches to religious truth in an intellectual situation marked by a pervasive sense of relativity.

The problem of making faith plausible is not new. It was Augustine who formulated it with the sharpest accuracy when he said: *"Nullus quippe credit aliquid, nisi prius cogitaverit esse credendum"*—"No one, indeed, believes anything, unless he previously knows it to be believable."[45] The only edge we may conceivably have today over Augustine in this insight is a more systematic awareness of the social dynamics of both *cogitatio* and *credenda*, of what is known and what is believed—an awareness that I discussed in terms of the sociology of knowledge in the section on plausibility structures. This new awareness, however, greatly increases the difficulty of simply submitting to tradition, and thus tends toward inductive modes of theological thought.

The theological method I have suggested here is strongly inclined toward an independent stance vis-à-vis the various religious traditions. But the problem of confronting the traditions remains, and no theological method is likely to be very productive unless it seriously faces this problem. Why? It is perhaps more useful to say why *not*. From the point of view presented in this book, the traditions must *not* be confronted because they have some mysterious but irresistible claim to our loyalty. Such notions have a curious persistence, even among intellectuals who have largely emancipated themselves from their respective religious backgrounds, but who nevertheless view the respective traditions as somehow part of the individual's being—an inner reality that he must confront. In the Western world, such an attitude is most frequently found among Jews, for historically understandable reasons. But among Christians, too, we come across such statements as "I must find out more about my faith," or, even more sharply, "I really ought to learn what we believe." The terms "faith" and "we" refer, of course, to the religious community from which the individual happens to come. Putting the matter this way illuminates the weakness in logic of the underlying attitude, whatever its *psychological* plausibility. Faith, in the proper meaning of the word, is or is not held. If it is, no "learning" is necessary; if it is not, one cannot refer to it as one's own. And the "we" of a religious community, which is by definition based on a religious faith held in common, cannot be logically taken as anteceding that faith except, perhaps, as a sociological proposition—but that is not what people who speak this way mean.

One can, of course, understand and sympathize with this attitude; there are often obvious, psychological reasons why people feel this way. There is even something touching about a Jewish agnostic who feels twitches of conscience as he eats his dinner on Yom Kippur, or a skeptic of Catholic antecedents who senses a pressure under his kneecaps as the host is carried by on Corpus Christi. If such psychological data are elevated to become criteria of truth, however, they become mystifications that perform the function Sartre called "bad faith"—that is, they misrepresent choice as destiny and thus deny the choices actually made. To be sure, such ideas as the eternal efficacy of "Jewish blood" or of the sacrament of baptism do much to give Jewishness or Christianity "indelible character." Once a Jew, always a Jew. Once baptized, forever a Christian. Ideas of this sort are, I think, essentially magical. Within the frame of reference suggested here, they must be interpreted as dehumanizing distortions of the empirical reality of our existence.

There are better reasons why the traditions must be confronted. On the most obvious level, the adage that "he who ignores history is condemned to repeat it" holds for the theologian as well. The fundamental questions of theology have been passionately considered for at least three thousand years. It is not only insufferable arrogance to think that one can begin theologizing in sovereign disregard of this history; it is also extremely uneconomical. It seems rather a waste of time to spend, say, five years working out a position, only to find that it has already been done by a Syrian monk in the fifth century. The very least that a knowledge of religious traditions has to offer is a catalogue of heresies for possible home use.

More importantly, though, the method I have been suggesting precludes turning away from history. If human experience contains theologically relevant data, the historical dimension of all human experience must be taken into account theologically. If there are genuine cases of the discovery of religious truth, we must come to grips with their history, for the very word "discovery" implies a historical process. This is even more clearly the case if we repudiate the idea of "progress." If all history were a steady progression, there might be a certain logic to ignoring the past. By definition, every past situation would in its approach to truth be inferior to the present. One would concern oneself with the past, if at all, simply for self-satisfied edification, in about the same mood as that of some early ethnologists' studies of "savages." But if, on the other hand, each age is seen in its "immediacy to God," each age must be carefully looked at for whatever signals of transcendence might be uniquely its own. To return to an earlier example, the theologian must concern himself with history because there is at least the possibility of his finding out about that one, never-to-be-repeated flash of truth which was the secret possession of a cabal of Aztec priests—and which might, who knows, provide the solution to his own most pressing problem.

By the same logic, this confrontation with the past cannot be limited to any one tradition, however much an individual may be personally attached to it. Theologizing today must take place in an ecumenical consciousness. In our present, pluralistic situation, it is becoming more and more difficult to stay religiously *entre nous*. All religious groups are constantly confronted by the massive presence of a secularized world view in its multiform manifestations and, on top of that, keep bumping into each other at every turn. Christian bumps into Jew, Catholic into Protestant, while the intra-Protestant bumping process has attained almost orgiastic intensity. With a little bit of luck one may even bump into the latest jet-propelled guru, fresh from the East with religious luggage of appropriately light weight for convenient air travel. Today everyone is forced into a permanent conversation with everyone else, which is mostly carried on in a very polite manner. It is funny, but, I daresay, it is also salutary. It is healthy for nuns to have to deal with rabbis, and vice versa, and it won't hurt either group to come up against a few Hindu holy men. In any case it is very difficult to ignore ecumenical consciousness, even if one desires to.

In this particular instance, the practical necessity is tantamount to a theoretical blessing. For an ecumenical consciousness makes possible a mode of theologizing that is very aware of the fullness of man's religious quest in a way that is probably unparalleled in the history of religion. It thus increases the likelihood that no genuine discovery of religious truth will be overlooked simply because of the accident of the theologian's birth.

The actual pressures of the pluralistic situation are further augmented by the unprecedented availability of the past as a result of modern historical scholarship. The contemporary theologian has within his reach an incredible wealth of information about man's religious thought in every known period of history—often in the form of inexpensive paper-backs! It is hard to see how intelligent use of this opportunity can fail to redound to the benefit of the theological enterprise. There is no longer any excuse for theological ethnocentrism.

It should today be inconceivable to carry on theological work without taking cognizance of this ecumenical abundance. Within the camp of Western Christianity, at least, this is coming to be generally accepted, and the ecumenical movement properly speaking has tried to bring Eastern Christianity more and more into the "polylogue" (if the term will be permitted). In America the conversation between Christianity and Judaism, too, has increasingly come to be regarded as a desirable exercise. But however much all this is to be welcomed, it is still too narrow a definition of ecumenical consciousness. After all, Christians and Jews are in the position of first cousins talking to each other. At the very least, they ought to draw into the conversation their second cousins from the House of Islam. And it is very much to be wished (and very probably inevitable) that the conversation be extended to include the great religious traditions of India and the Far East, both as they presently exist and as they are available in the respective literatures. It should not be necessary to belabor the point that this desideratum is implied in the particular method I have suggested.

Ecumenical consciousness should be more than a response to practical necessities or an accommodation to intercultural good manners as practiced in the United Nations delegates' lounge. It is not a question of becoming sophisticated about or polite to people who, say, worship cows or are worried about swatting flies. It is a question of seriously attempting an inductive approach to the theological enterprise. One point should, however, be strongly emphasized. I am *not* recommending the construction of a catchall system, a sort of theological Esperanto in which all traditions will be dissolved. On the contrary, ecumenical consciousness should be particularly conducive to the clarification of contradictory options. Only when these options have become fully conscious will it be possible to understand them as *available choices*. In other words, only an ecumenically conscious theology is in the position of really being able to make choices—be they choices between historically available traditions, or choices that modify these traditions, or perhaps a choice to strike out in new directions in opposition to all the traditions. For example, any attempt to blend Christianity and Buddhism is almost certainly based on ignorance of one or both of these traditions. Christianity and Buddhism present us with clear and, I think, essentially contradictory religious options. The protagonists of both religions should be clear about what both options are, and so should the people who choose neither religion. Almost inevitably, the knowledge of these historical options will enrich the intellectual clarity of the individual's own choice.

These ideas are by no means new. They were very common during the heyday of Protestant theological liberalism and were a powerful factor in the growth of the historical and comparative study of religion during the same period. There was at the time a very strong expectation in scholarly circles and among laymen that this kind of engagement with the wealth of man's religious quest, past and present, would enable men to make more rational choices in this area. One may recall here by way of examples the immense effort that went into Max Müller's compilation of the *Sacred Books of the East* and, on the popular side, the excitement generated in the 1890s by the World Parliament of Religions, held in conjunction with the Chicago World's Fair. The scholarly achievements of this era are monumental and even today form the indispensable foundation for almost all work in the history of religion. But we would do well not to be too blasé about the less scholarly manifestations of this "premature ecumenism." I am not suggesting that one should be terribly impressed by little old ladies in tennis shoes rushing about to proclaim "*Ex oriente lux*" with a Midwestern accent (though, I confess, I find them considerably more impressive than intellectuals of any accent who are convinced that no light can come from anywhere outside their own depressing cliques). But even this kind of popularizing activity (I mean, of course, the little old ladies, not the intellectuals' cliques) can serve as an important part of the plausibility structure of an intellectually more serious enterprise.

I am not, as I stressed earlier, suggesting a simple return to an earlier period of religious thought either. In religion as in anything else it is almost never possible to return to an earlier state of affairs. Nor would I want to. I certainly would not want to revive the shallow faith in progress, the dreary rationalism, or the smug self-satisfaction of the *belle époque*, even if it were feasible. But, to repeat, I *would* want to revive a deeper motif of what has justly been called the Schleiermacher era—a spirit of patient induction and an attitude of openness to the fullness of human experience, especially as this experience is accessible to historical inquiry.

The traditions, *all* the traditions, must be confronted in search of whatever signals of transcendence may have been sedimented in them. This means an approach grounded in empirical methods of inquiry (most importantly, of course, in the methods of modern historical scholarship) and free of dogmatic a prioris (free, that is, of the dogmatic assumptions of the neo-orthodox reaction). A few years ago a group of younger Protestant theologians in Germany published a collective work, intended as a sharp challenge to neo-orthodoxy and provocatively entitled *Revelation as History*.[46] The key figure in this group is Wolfhart Pannenberg, whose work continues to emphasize both empirical history and empirical anthropology. I strongly endorse this approach. But I would prefer an emphasis on "discovery" as against "revelation." To be sure, if one has already achieved faith, one will see any manifestation of transcendence as a revelation or, as Mircea

Eliade puts it, a "theophany." But it is precisely this "already achieved" status that I would like to get away from in terms of theological method, at least in its starting point. To speak of "revelation" before one is sure just where one may speak of "discovery" is putting the cart before the horse.[47]

History provides us with the record of man's experience with himself and with reality. This record contains those experiences, in a variety of forms, that I have called signals of transcendence. The theological enterprise will have to be first of all, a rigorously empirical analysis of these experiences, in terms of both a historical anthropology and a history of religion, and, if my suggestion is followed, the former will have logical priority over the latter. The theological enterprise will go beyond the empirical frame of reference at the point where it begins to speak of discoveries and to explicate what is deemed to have been discovered—that is, at the point where the transcendent intentions in human experience are treated as *realities* rather than as *alleged realities*.

Needless to say, this transition from empirical analysis to metaphysics is in itself an act of faith. Only in the anticipation of such faith will theology separate itself from the empirical study of man and his religious productions. And only then will it become theology in the etymologically proper sense of the word. Thus it is absurd to speak of a "scientific theology" (as, for example, has been the tendency in Scandinavia, particularly in Sweden, where theology has been virtually absorbed in the phenomenology and history of religion). In any empirical frame of reference, transcendence must appear as a projection of man. Therefore, if transcendence is to be spoken of *as* transcendence, the empirical frame of reference must be left behind. It cannot be otherwise. My concern is the method by which this switch in frames of reference is to be attained.

An example may make this clearer. Much has been made in recent Protestant theology of the centralness of Christ and the alleged necessity of starting the theological enterprise with the figure of Christ. At its worst, this approach systematizes the rape of the historical materials, as when Christian beliefs are read back into the religious history of ancient Israel. But even at its most sophisticated, when history is treated carefully and respectfully, it means that all theological interpretations of historical materials should emanate from this one central focus, which is itself taken as an unchanging a priori. I repudiate such a procedure. I would take the historical materials concerning Christ, both the New Testament itself and the subsequent literature, as a record of a specific complex of human experience. As such, it has no special position as against any comparable record (say, the record concerning the Buddha in the Pali canon and the subsequent ramifications of Buddhist thought). The questions I would then ask would be essentially the same as on any other record: *What is being said here? What is the human experience out of which these statements come?* And then: *To what extent, and in what way, may we see here genuine discoveries of transcendent truth?*

I must leave aside the question whether, in this particular instance, this approach calls for a renewal of the "quest for the historical Jesus," as some New Testament scholars have recently urged, or whether we must remain satisfied with the position of the Bultmann school that the historical Jesus remains inaccessible and that, willy-nilly, we are stuck with the Christ proclaimed as divine savior by the early church. This question exceeds both my scope and my competence. It is the methodological question that interests me here. I would go back to the classical *modus operandi* of nineteenth-century biblical scholarship. I would also go back to the spirit of relentless honesty, which is not so much disrespectful of established religious authority as ruthless with one's own religious hopes. Protestantism, the first religious tradition that found the courage to turn the sharp instruments of empirical inquiry back upon itself, has good reason to be proud of this spirit. In this sense (and not in the sense of an a priori commitment to a particular tradition) the procedure I am suggesting partakes of the "living, moving restless power" of what Paul Tillich called "the Protestant principle": "Protestantism has a principle that stands beyond all its realizations. . . . The Protestant principle is the judge of every religious and cultural reality, including the religion and culture which calls itself 'Protestant.' "[48] In this sense, and in this sense only, the approach I would take to the phenomenon of Christ is unabashedly Protestant. The "judgment" that is implied in this approach is as far as can be from self-satisfied arrogance in the face of the religious ecstasies of man. On the contrary, it is animated by patient openness and humility before all available intimations of religious truth.

I have in this chapter emphasized the necessity for the theological enterprise to confront the religious traditions, both those of the theologian's own cultural and biographical background and those that are foreign to it. I hope I have made clear that this does not contradict what I said in the preceding chapter about an anthropological starting point for theology. I am not now substituting historical scholarship for anthropology in the recommended starting point. I am, however, suggesting that the theological enterprise ought to entail confrontations of more than one kind. In addition to the confrontation with what can be empirically discovered about man and his works (which will be, above all, a confrontation with philosophical anthropology and with the socio-historical sciences of man), there must also be the confrontation with the contents of all the religious traditions both within and beyond one's own cultural milieu. There may also be the need to confront insights into man's reality from yet other sources, such as those the artist and the poet draw from. The search for signals of transcendence within human experience will hardly be able to afford to overlook such data as derive from, for instance, the creations of Bach or Mozart, of Gothic cathedral builders, or of Chagall, Hölderlin, or Blake (to mention names at random). As yet, we can barely conceive of the procedures by which this particular confrontation might be realized.

It is hardly staggering news to suggest that theology should engage in a many-sided conversation with other intellectual disciplines, certainly not in a situation in which the word "dialogue" has become a fashionable cliché. Nor would the substitution of the term "polylogue" be a worthwhile improvement. Everything, however, depends upon the manner in which this many-sided conversation is carried on, and a good deal will depend on the motives with which it is entered. There is no need to reiterate my earlier strictures on the motives of "with-it-ness" and of gaining the attention of the latest coterie of "cultured despisers of religion" to be picked up by the mass media. Any motive other than the search for truth degrades theology, as it degrades any other intellectual enterprise. Even the motive of pastoral or evangelistic concern is no exception to this. But the manner of confrontation is of decisive importance. "Dialogue" can be an alibi for charlatanism, in which everybody talks to everybody and nobody has anything to say. The so-called dynamics of communication can never be a substitute for the hard labor of intellectual effort. But "dialogue" can also be an inner necessity of a particular intellectual situation. Then it is undertaken with no other motive except the search for truth and not as a putative short cut to insights that can be obtained only by rigorous application. This I would welcome as one of the most promising possibilities of our contemporary situation. I also think that theologizing in this attitude can be one of the most exciting intellectual activities in this situation.

At the same time it must be recognized that religion is not primarily an activity of intellectuals, indeed cannot be understood as a primarily theoretical endeavor. The fundamental religious impulse is not to theorize about transcendence but to worship it. This is so regardless of whether religion animates large numbers of people in a society or is limited to what I have called cognitive minorities. If religion in our situation could manifest itself only as a theoretical concern, however passionate, of segments of the intelligentsia, this would in itself be a symptom of its progressive or impending demise. Any such intellectualism is particularly repugnant to the Judaeo-Christian traditions, in which faith has always been understood in relation to the actual life, work, and hope of human communities that include ditchdiggers as well as theoreticians. I therefore recognize that the theological enterprise I am speaking of, even if it employs the most complex tools of the intellectual's trade, will always push toward expression in living communities of men other than intellectuals. It would be foolhardy to speculate on the social forms that such communities might eventually take. But it is possible to extend the concept of pluralism to such communities. Some of them may well emerge within the traditional religious groupings or institutions, as new variants of the classical type of the *ecclesiola in ecclesia* (the "little church within the church," as a more intimate grouping within the larger community). There are already indications of this possibility in a variety of groups that (probably misleadingly) have been subsumed under the phrase "underground churches." Other such communities may congeal outside the lines drawn in our society by the religious institutions, outside the gates of the churches and possibly with little or no connection with the latter's traditional contents. Examples of this already exist too. Whether these communities tend toward "sectarian" or "churchly" (or, in the American context, "denominational") social forms will depend, as we have seen, upon the degree to which their contents deviate from the cognitive consensus of the over-all society. In either eventuality, as long as the religious contents are "living" rather than "dead," the communities embodying them will be communities of practice as well as theory. The practice may take different forms (conceivably political forms as well), but one form that will inevitably reappear, because of the intrinsic nature of man's religion, is worship. It is in worship that the prototypical gesture of religion is realized again and again. This is the gesture in which man reaches out in hope toward transcendence.

Unavoidably both this chapter and the preceding one have turned out to contain programs. Under ideal circumstances I would have had to wait until, say, the tenth anniversary of my retirement before I would have been in a position to present even a rough design of these programs. I must confess to a rather American lack of patience with such intellectual asceticism. But I must also confess to being very susceptible to another American propensity, to wit, the feeling that people should put up or shut up. Being unwilling (evidently) to shut up, and being unable to put up to the desired degree, I would still like to venture a few steps beyond program-making. Just as I earlier attempted to indicate what an anthropological starting point for theology might mean, so I ought properly to conclude this chapter with at least some indications of how the traditions might be confronted in terms of the theological program I have suggested. For obvious reasons of economy, these remarks will be limited to the Christian tradition.[49]

One possibility would be a differentiated approach to the tradition. With regard to some elements of the tradition I can see a strong reaffirmation of their classical formulations, a reaffirmation *adversus modernos*, ''against the moderns,'' in the teeth of secularized consciousness. With regard to other elements, I can see only the possibility of extracting certain discoveries from their classical context and starting anew the task of theological formulation. My approach would thus be ''heretical'' in the strict sense of the word—a theological stance marked by selectivity vis-à-vis the tradition. I will leave it to others to assign my selections to this or that entry in the voluminous catalogue of ancient heresies that every dogmatician seems to carry around in his head. Apart from the pleasure of recognition that may be obtained from stumbling upon ideological buddies in, say, ancient

Alexandria or Antioch, such assignments can be of serious significance only to the orthodox.

Adversus modernos, I would, above all, reaffirm the conception of God that emerged in the religious experience of ancient Israel and that is available to us in the literature of the Old Testament. It is possible, with all deliberation and with full awareness of the immense cross-cultural range of human religion, to speak here of *a discovery of God*. The God whom Israel discovered (in its own self-understanding, of course, it was this God who revealed Himself to Israel) was an unheard-of novelty in the context of the religious world of the ancient Near East. He was the God who was wholly other with regard to the "natural" reality of human experience, not to be found either within man (as in the orgiastic religions of the surrounding cultures) or within the world (as in any conception of a necessary connection between a divinity and a particular people). He stood outside man and outside the world, yet He was also the creator of both man and world. His sovereign transcendence and otherness did not, however, imply indifference or inaccessibility to the reality of human experience. On the contrary, this God is encountered as a God who speaks to man and whose manifestations are to be sought, above all, in the historical events of human experience. And God's speaking to man takes, first and foremost, the form of an overpowering ethical demand.

In its central conception of God the biblical tradition (in which, in this respect, we ought to include not only Judaism and Christianity, but most definitely also Islam, with its violent protest against any dilutions of the transcendent majesty of God) is set off sharply against the great religious traditions of India and the Far East, and also against the this-worldliness and neo-mysticism of modern Western secularism, which, whenever it becomes restless in its prison house, can look for an escape only in one or another expedition into the alleged depths of human consciousness itself (as in the various forms of contemporary psychological salvation). Mysticism, broadly speaking, is any religious practice or doctrine that asserts the ultimate unity of man and the divine. This fundamental quality of mysticism has been classically formulated in Hinduism by the formula *tat tvam asi*—"thou art that," that is, the depths of the human soul are identical with the divine depths of the universe. Mystical religion, therefore, always looks for salvation within the putative depths of human consciousness itself. This is why the term "neo-mysticism" fits much of what goes on today under the banner of psychotherapy. All these quests for salvation from within are diametrically opposed to the biblical conception of God as one standing outside and against man.

The God of the biblical tradition is the polar antithesis of the great identity proclaimed by the mystics, and of any possible variation on this theme. To reaffirm this discovery of God in our situation might necessitate the formulation of new creeds, though their content would in this case be quite traditional—the reaffirmation of God who is not the world and who was not made by man, who is outside and not within ourselves, who is not a sign of human things but of whom human things are signs, who is symbolized and not a symbol. It is *this* God, totally other and yet accessible in human experience, in whom faith will see the foundation of order, justice, and compassion in the world. It is *this* transcendence of which certain human gestures in the world are signals. And it is the faith in *this* God that (as it did in the religious history of Israel) eventuates in a hope that reaches beyond the confines of death.

These affirmations are Jewish or Muslim as much as they are Christian. In terms of the classical Christian creeds, they refer to the first rather than the second or third article of faith. It is with respect to these latter strata in the tradition that I would find a new theological venture more plausible than a reformation of traditional orthodoxies. If one can, indeed, speak of a discovery of Christ as one can of a discovery of God, then I see the link between the two in the agonizing problem of theodicy. All Christology is concerned with salvation. To speak of Christ is to speak of man's redemption, even in the seemingly most abstruse Christological controversies. For instance, some modern commentators have been amused by the violent debates in the early church as to whether God and Christ are to be understood as *homoiousion* ("of similar substance") or as *homoousion* ("of the same substance")—all this commotion over one letter! But in this one Greek letter *iota* rested the whole question of how Christ could be the hope for man's salvation. The *homoousion* formula was finally accepted by the church, not because of some esoteric philosophical logic, but because it was necessary to faith to affirm that it was God, and truly God, who was incarnate in Christ, suffered, and rose again for man's salvation.

A quest for redemption is by no means the prerogative of the biblical tradition. One has only to recall the importance of the idea of *moksha* (release from the sorrows of existence) in the religious formulations of ancient India. And despite the vast differences in the conceptions of just what man is to be redeemed from and how this might be accomplished (as, say, between a biblical conception of man's sin and the Hindu view of man's predicament), there is a common, empirically given human reality that underlies all quests for redemption. This is the reality of suffering, of evil, and of death.

To be sure, there is an immense difference between Job's perplexity about his misfortune in the context of a belief in the omnipotence of God and the Buddha's reflection about the roots of human suffering in the context of a belief in the endless wheel of rebirths. But the empirical reality of suffering in ancient Israel and ancient India could not have been very different. The begging leper, who was one of the four sights that led the young Buddha To retire from the world and seek redemption, must have looked very much like that afflicted Israelite, covered "with loathsome sores from the sole of his foot to the crown of his head" (Job 2:7).

The agonizing question about the ultimate meaning of human suffering and evil is, however, immeasurably aggravated by the conception of God in the biblical tradition. The discovery of the one God, all-powerful and all-good, creator of the world and sovereign of history, had to raise the question of theodicy in its sharpest possible form. All Christology, I believe, is at root an answer to this question.

The discovery of Christ implies the discovery of the redeeming presence of God within the anguish of human experience. Now God is perceived not only in terrible confrontation with the world of man, but present within it as suffering love. This presence makes possible the ultimate vindication of the creation, and thus the reconciliation between the power and the goodness of the creator. By the same token, it vindicates the hope that human suffering has redeeming significance. The history of man comes to be seen as one vast movement toward the moment when this vindication will become manifest (in the language of the New Testament, when the Kingdom of God will have finally come). In Christ, however, this final vindication is anticipated. Redemption is yet to come, as the world "in this eon" is still dominated by suffering, evil, and death. But redemption is already present here and now because, hidden within the empirical reality of the world, the essential work of redemption has already been accomplished. This *presence* of redemption is accessible to faith here and now, not only in the hope for the coming consummation. It is this duality of anticipation and presentness that sets off Christian faith, on the one hand from the timeless ecstasy of all mysticism, on the other hand from the grim imprisonment in history of all this-worldly doctrines of salvation (notably the Marxist one).

To this extent, of course, such a Christological formulation is amenable to incorporation within this or that orthodox position. Where it becomes hopelessly heterodox is in its omission of the historical reference to that Jesus who was crucified under Pontius Pilate. It can hardly be doubted that it was in connection with the events surrounding the life of Jesus that this new understanding of God's relationship to man emerged. This is admitted by both those who want to root Christian faith in the historical figure and those who would see only the figure as witnessed to (and, presumably, transformed) in the message of the early church. However important may be the findings of historical scholarship on these events, I find it difficult to see how, in the wake of all the relativizations of which we must take cognizance today, an inductive faith can rest upon the exclusive authority of these events—and thus, how the discovery of Christ as the redeeming presence of God in the world can be exclusively linked to the figure of the historical Jesus. If *this* exclusiveness is to be identified with the much-vaunted historical character of Christian faith, then perhaps this particular historical character will have to be left behind in favor of a more ecumenical one. With this heterodox *haeresis*, however, the exclusiveness of the Christian tradition will be relativized in the second as well as the third article of faith (the articles about Christ and the church), as classically formulated.

I see Christ as historically manifested in Jesus but not historically given (as the splendidly defiant particularity of the creedal phrase "under Pontius Pilate" or the all too precise specificity of the dating of events surrounding the birth of Jesus in Luke 3:1–2 suggest). In other words, the redeeming presence of God in the world is manifested in history, but it is not given once and for all in the particular historical events reported on in the New Testament. I am then constrained to disregard the insistence of the New Testament authors that redemption lies only "in this name" of Jesus Christ (that is, the name that links the historical figure with the cosmic scope of God's redeeming presence). This

leads on to the affirmation that while Christ can be and has been
"named," He is not identical with any name—an affirmation
close to those Christian heresies that de-emphasized the historical
Jesus as against the cosmic Christ, redeemer of all possible
worlds. But I would not wish to share in the turning from history
and in the pessimism of many of these heresies (notably, of
course, the Gnostic ones).

It follows that the community (or, more exactly, communities)
in which Christ becomes manifest cannot be identified with any
particular "names" or traditions, though He may be more manifest in some than in others. The presence of Christ will have to
be determined not by a direct succession from a certain point in
the past, but rather from such evidence as can be found in the
empirical reality of communities whose actions can be called
redemptive. Wherever communities gather around acts of redeeming love, there we may look for the presence of Christ. The
redemptive community of Christ in the world must be seen as
ever coming into being again in the empirical history of man. It
will be there implicitly wherever the redeeming gestures of love,
hope, and compassion are reiterated in human experience. It will
become explicit wherever these gestures are understood in relation
to the God who both created and redeems the world, who may
well have been "in Jesus," but who is ever again present in the
human imitations of redemptive love. Every such community,
whether implicitly in its actions or explicitly in its worship, an-
ticipates here and now the consummation of redemption toward
which the world is moving.

I am well aware of the fact that, in the attempt to show how
an inductive theological position might confront a particular religious tradition, I have swung wildly to right and left, cutting
through a multitude of Gordian knots carefully tied together in
centuries of theological cerebration. Each statement in the preceding paragraphs, to be properly defended (or, as the Germans
so nicely put it, "protected"), would require a book at least as

long as this one. I plead guilty to the charge of "terrible simplification." It could be, though, that a certain kind of simplification is long overdue in the business of theologizing. I hope that it is the simplification not of ignorance, but of an effort to get at basic questions. The point could also be made that many new intellectual departures have become possible only after the luxuriant complexities accumulated before them have once more been reduced to surveyable simplicity.

5

A Lutheran View of the Elephant*

Let me begin by saying that I'm honored and pleased to be speaking here under the auspices of the Inter-Lutheran Forum. Most of my public speaking of late, for some reason, has been under Roman Catholic auspices, my Lutheran credentials are becoming quite doubtful, and it is time that I do something to refurbish them. Maybe this will do it. But I should tell you in all candor that my acceptance of the invitation to speak here was not motivated solely by an eruption of my underground Lutheran identity. I was told that my presentation this evening should have a light touch, perhaps even be witty; but that it should also be serious, perhaps even theological; and, of course, that it should have a Lutheran angle. Frankly, this was a challenge that I would have found difficult to turn down. So, here I am; I could do no other—not, at any rate, without looking upon myself as an escapist from what may well be the most formidable assignment of my career as a public speaker.

*Inter-Lutheran Forum, Advent 1978

The assignment immediately made me think of a classic Jewish joke. (Almost all classic jokes are Jewish, of course. One of the most urgent tasks before anyone embarking on the Christian-Jewish dialogue that is so much called for today is a theological inquiry into the structure of Jewish humor. I'm *not* being witty; I'm being very serious. But, alas, this is not the topic I'm going to address myself to today.) It seems that there was an international competition for the best book on the elephant. The German entry was a three-volume scientific treatise on the nervous system of the elephant; the French entry was a slim erotic novel about elephants; the British contribution was entitled *Reminiscences of Elephant-Hunting Days in Tanganyika*; the Russian entry *The Elephant: Does He Exist?* and the American entry *Bigger and Better Elephants*. The Jewish contribution had the title *The Elephant and the Jewish Problem*. As I said, I thought of this joke as soon as I was given my marching orders for tonight. From then on, it was a matter of free association. In view of an upcoming anniversary that is being drummed up in some publications that may be familiar to you, I first thought of giving my address the title "The Elephant and the Unaltered Augsburg Confession." But this, I thought, would be pushing it a bit. Consequently, my title tonight is, more modestly, "A Lutheran View of the Elephant."

The elephant has always occupied a particular place in the human imagination. And no wonder: Since the extinction of the giant reptiles, it has been the largest animal on earth. It has impressed itself on the human mind by its enormous size, its power, its outlandish form. It made its first appearance in Europe, as far as I know, when Hannibal climbed the Alps with his war elephants, striking terror into Roman hearts and contributing the adjective "elephantine" to a sequence of Latin-derived languages. Europeans, it appears, were willing to believe almost anything about this animal. Thus Strabo informs us that the male elephant, copulating in a ferocious frenzy, impregnates the female by "discharging a kind of fatty matter through the breathing-hole which he has beside his temples." (I'm conscious of addressing an audience of Lutherans, schooled in *Wissenschaftlichkeit*, so I better give you the reference for this: It is from the fifteenth book of the *Geography*, chapter 1, section 43, and I quoted from the translation by Horace Leonard Jones, London 1930. As to Strabo's *Wissenschaftlichkeit*, the passage hardly speaks for it, as any observant visitor to the Bronx Zoo will agree. But let that pass.) Outside Europe, of course, wherever elephants have been more than occasional invaders, elephantine imagery has been much more prominent. The elephant is a sacred animal in any number of African cultures. It graces the coat of arms of Thailand to this day. There are myths and legends about it all over southern and southeast Asia. And in India, the elephant is the form of one of the most popular divinities, Ganesh or Ganesha, who is also an important and recurring theme in Indian art.

The enormity of the elephant is awe-inspiring. Like all enormous things, it is also comic. Indeed, our English word "enormity" suggests both huge size and an outlandishness that provokes laughter. Let me only observe in passing that it is no accident that the term "elephantiasis" is given to a disease in which one part of the human anatomy swells into a huge size, and that Africans, despite the horror of the disease, also find the spectacle funny. (I don't think that this fact should be interpreted as cruelty, but I cannot pursue this here.)

But let us come back closer to home. The enormous size of the elephant serves as a comic device to point up various enormities of ordinary social life. The enormity of the advertiser, for instance, who is prepared to make any claim, however absurd, for his product: How does one seat four elephants in a Volkswagen? Easy; two in front, two in back. Or the enormity of the capitalist ethic in general, as in the joke about the American tourist in India. An Indian is trying to sell him an elephant, supposedly a great bargain at $800. The American doesn't want to buy, points out that he lives in New York City, on the eighteenth floor of a high rise, in a small two-room apartment. The Indian keeps going down in price—$750-$700-$600—the American still says no. Finally, the Indian says: "Ah, sahib. I can see that you are a hard bargainer. I will make you my last offer: *Two* elephants, at $650." And the American tourist (the guy who lives on the eighteenth floor in the studio on East Seventy-third Street) says: "*Now* you're talking!"

But let me rather tell you what I think is the *Ur*-elephant-joke, to be found, I believe, in the lost eighth book of the *Ramayana*, the great Hindu epic about the endless love affair between Rama and Sita. A mouse comes upon an elephant. The mouse is male, the elephant female. The elephant is in a good mood and looks down benignly upon the mouse: "Hello, little mouse. I am so big and you are so small. That is very funny. I like you, little mouse." The mouse takes courage from this and says: "Oh, Miss Elephant, you are really very nice. Let me tell you a wish I have had for many, many years. I have always wanted to make love to an elephant. Will you let me?" The elephant laughs uproariously, slaps her hindlegs with her trunk, and says: "Sure. Go ahead, little mouse." The elephant lies down under a coconut tree and accommodates herself to the mouse as best as she can. The mouse enthusiastically gets busy fulfilling his old wish. The elephant, of course, hardly notices what is going on there, and eventually falls asleep. But after a minute or so a gust of wind moves through the trees, a coconut falls off and hits the elephant on the head. The elephant wakes up and exclaims, "*Ouch!*" Whereupon the mouse says solicitously: "Oh, I'm sorry. Did I hurt you?"

What are we to make of all this? Well, there is one central tradition in modern Western thought that serves to illuminate all this elephantine symbolism. It is the tradition of understanding all symbol systems as projections of the human situation. Ludwig

Feuerbach put this understanding in classical form, but there are many variations of it. The root phenomenon is the human capacity to infuse meaning into the world and, more specifically, to let non-human realities represent (that is, symbolize) human realities. Thus, in every one of our elephant jokes, the elephant represents or symbolizes this or that human reality. Such a human reality can be collective or individual, and the symbolism of the comic can be successfully understood as a projection of both social and psychological concerns. Freud, of course, gave us the paradigmatic psychology of the comic in his book *Jokes and Their Relation to the Unconscious*. Marxists are, apparently without exception, utterly humorless, but if a Marxist theoretician with a sense of humor should ever appear, he will have no difficulty formulating a Marxist theory of the comic in terms of the projection of class struggle, false consciousness and the like. Now, one may quarrel with the details of Freudian or Marxist theory—I certainly do—but it is important to emphasize that the fundamental insight of Feuerbach (the granddaddy of Freudians as well as Marxists) is fully valid: Man is indeed the great projectionist, the symbol-maker. Not satisfied with organizing his own individual and collective life in terms of symbolic representations (the most basic of which, of course, is human language), he projects his symbols into the cosmos. This is but another way of saying that man *humanizes* the cosmos—or, to use an older term, man views the universe from an anthropomorphic perspective.

Jokes humanize the universe. So does religion. Feuerbach brilliantly understood this, and he followed up this insight in his program of reducing theology to anthropology, a program that has provided the agenda for philosophers, psychologists and social thinkers for the last hundred and fifty years. It is probably no exaggeration to say that the Feuerbachian reduction has also been the central theme of Christian, especially Protestant, theologians during the same period, no matter whether they assented to the program or sought to repudiate it. Let there be no doubt about this, however, the comic and the mythical elephants are the products of the human mind; they are *our* elephants. We thought them up, and in doing so we fill them with contents derived from our own being and our own situation. Put another way: The figure of Ganesh is a human symbol. Just *what* it symbolizes may be disputed—the unresolved Oedipus complex of Brahmin child-rearing, the contradictions of the caste system, or, who knows, the mythopoetic propensities of Sanskrit grammar. No one should waste his time disputing *that* the figure is a symbol.

Whatever you may think of the way I got here, you will have to agree that I have gotten to theology, as instructed. So, let me state where I have arrived more succinctly: The gods are projections of the human mind. The gods are symbols of the human condition. Consequently, religion can be successfully analyzed as a human symbol-system—historically, sociologically, psychologically and linguistically. Consequently, any theology that denies this (be it orthodox, neo-orthodox or what-have-you) is a dead-end street. One gets nowhere, in theology as in any other pursuit, if one's starting point is a denial of demonstrable empirical reality.

But this is not the whole story. The question of whether religion is an assemblage of human symbols has been definitely answered, and answered positively. In that sense, Marx was perfectly right when, playing on the German meaning of Feuerbach's name, he said that everyone must pass through this "fiery brook." The trouble with Marx's theory of religion is that he did *not* pass through the brook, but rather got stuck in it—as did Freud, as did Nietzsche, as still do regiments of contemporary Christian theologians. But there is an additional question, actually a very simple one. If religion is an assemblage of human symbols, *is this all it is*?

Let me tell you a story. One of Marco Polo's regrettably lesser known colleagues was the great Venetian traveler Giacomo Granbocca. (Go ahead, look him up. He was the author of the work entitled *Miracoli dell' India*, which you may peruse in the English translation of the Rev. H. H. Shuttleworth, Glastonbury, Connecticut, 1834). Chapter 81 of Granbocca's *Miracoli* contains a long dissertation on Indian elephants. In this he tells us, among other things, that the female elephant kills the male immediately after impregnation and that elephants will stomp to death any one of their number who would set himself up as a leader over them. Now, as we learn from Shuttleworth's scholarly preface to the *Miracoli*, Granbocca was both a eunuch and a political exile. Not that Shuttleworth could have done it, repressed and reactionary nineteenth-century Congregationalist that he was, but you should have no difficulty coming up with a Freudian and a Marxist interpretation of Granbocca's elephant accounts: Granbocca's elephants were projections or symbols of Granbocca's psychosexual and sociopolitical problems. Indeed, if you try a little harder, you will be able to interpret his entire work in those terms. In other words, you will be able to deal with this work as if it did not deal with India at all, but with the mind and the life of its author. At that point, however, you will have overextended the interpretation. Take it from me that there are other statements made by Granbocca about India, even some of his other statements about elephants, which have been corroborated by other reports. That is, there are *some* things that Granbocca tells us about India that (never mind his sexual and political fantasies) stand up as facts. What your overly symbolist interpretation leaves out is this: India is a real place, Granbocca was there, and there are elephants in India.

Let me put this in more general terms: Both comedy and religion are human symbolizations, but both also have ontological intentionality. Both imply an access to objective realities in the world outside the human mind. I think that the two spheres of the comic and the religious are profoundly related to each other.

In any case, to say that the gods are human symbols is the beginning, not the end, of the process of reflecting about them. Any entity can serve as a symbol for any other entity, but that capacity to symbolize does not *ipso facto* say anything about the ontological status of the symbolizing entity (nor, for that matter, of the symbolized one). If this is conceded, a quite new avenue of exploration opens up. We can now ask, Do the gods exist, apart from their capacity to symbolize the human condition? If so, how are we to assess the accounts that have been given of them? And further, could it be that the gods actually manifest themselves within the human condition? Even a hypothetically positive reply to this last question would do precisely to Feuerbach what Marx did to Hegel—to wit, stand him on his head. For suddenly the symbolizer would appear as symbol, the projectionist as projection. At this juncture my argument becomes a little heavy. It is high time I get back to elephants.

In the telling of some of these elephant jokes, I stressed the hugeness of the elephant. Take another variant of the *Ur*-elephant-joke: An elephant and a mouse are crossing a bridge. When they get across, the mouse exclaims: "Boy, did we make that bridge shake!" But size is always relative. The elephant is huge when compared to a mouse, or to a man. But I would venture the interpretation that in these jokes, man is represented by the mouse, not the elephant. And the elephant, in turn, represents a hugeness much vaster than even that of this particular empirical animal. We should once again think of Ganesh. And here, I will stick my neck out. The elephant, I would contend, represents the vastness of the universe in which man finds himself. The enormity at issue, then, is finally cosmic. And in this context one must also see those other aspects of the elephant—its grotesqueness, even its absurdity. If this is so, can we learn anything from all this—*not* about man this time around, but perhaps about the cosmos?

There was once an international congress of philosophers. An Indian philosopher is talking to an American: "You Westerners have a completely wrong idea about the universe. You believe that the earth is a ball moving around the sun. That is a great mistake. Actually, the earth is a flat disc supported on the back of an enormous elephant." "Well, that's very interesting," says the American, "but what supports the elephant?" "There is a second elephant under the first," replies the Indian. "And what supports the second elephant?" "Ah yes, there is a third elephant supporting the second." And just as the American is about to make another objection the Indian says: "My good chap, you may as well face it: There are elephants *all the way*."

And then there was a young American who was on a pilgrimage to the Orient in order to discover the secret of life. He was told that high up in the Himalayas there was a holy man who would have the answer. After many weeks of arduous climbing and many hardships the young American finally reached the peak on which the holy man was sitting, immobile, in a perpetual trance. "Sir," said the young American, "my name is John P. Schulze, I'm from Cleveland, Ohio, and I have traveled all over the world to discover the secret of life. I understand that you know the secret. Would you please tell it to me?" The holy man came out of his trance and said: "*Life is a gigantic elephant turd.*" The young American puzzled over this for a moment, then asked: "A gigantic elephant turd? Are you sure about this?" "Of course not," said the holy man. "Do you have any other suggestions?"

All these elephant jokes hinge on discrepancy. As Henri Bergson correctly pointed out, discrepancy is at the heart of the comic phenomenon. (He was only wrong, I think, about the nature of the discrepancy. He thought it was between the animated and the mechanical elements in reality; I argue that this interpretation is too narrow.) The essence of the comic discrepancy is the disproportion between man and the universe into which he is thrown. Assuming this to be so, then the comic is more than a projection of human subjectivity. It is also, and far more importantly, a mode of perception. In other words, the comic has the quality of cognition, mediating insights into the objective constitution of reality. In this cognitive quality, the comic is very closely related to religion. For at the heart of the religious phenomenon also lies the experience of discrepancy between man and universe—be it a matter of absolute dependency (Schleiermacher), the adjustment to an unseen order (William James) the shattering encounter with the *mysterium tremendum* (Rudolf Otto), or simply the dichotomization of reality into the sacred and the profane. But the affinity of the comic and the religious goes beyond this cognitive structure. In both instances there is also a liberation, a redemptive quality to the cognitive insights. Laughter redeems. Indeed, I would be bold to say that each joke is, in its essence, a vignette of salvation. Laughter dies away, the joke comes to an end. The redemption of the comic is momentary, transitory, very fragile. But in the transitory moments ruled by the comic, it illuminates, in a flash, the ultimate fate of man's relation to the universe. That fate is liberating laughter. And this insight, of course, is religious in the most precise sense of the word.

The discrepancy is the human condition, accurately described by Pascal as the midpoint between the infinite and the nothing. Always one breath away from the nothing, man confronts the infinite. Come to think of it, what better image is there of man's trying to come to terms with the universe than that of a mouse trying to make love to an elephant? The elephant, because of its distinctive status in the zoological realm, is what might well be called a natural symbol of that infinite which man both confronts and reaches out toward. It is vast, powerful, grotesque in its proportions, reducing other elements of reality to absurdity. Above all, it is totally different from man, meta-human, *other*. Or, as Otto put it in his phenomenology of the experience of the sacred, it is *ex toto aliter*. Yet (and here is the profound paradox of all religious experience) this *other* manifests itself *here*, in this world ("here below," as Mircea Eliade puts it). Or, if you prefer the temporal categories of Biblical thought over spatial symbolism (I think that the difference between these two types of symbolic expression has been greatly exaggerated), the *other*, toward which all time moves, manifests itself *now*, "in this aeon." The infinite, the totally other is manifested here and now, in the empirical world of human existence, and that manifestation is a promise of redemption. *This* is the common experience of the comic and the religious, of *homo ridens* and of *homo religiosus*.

These considerations, it will perhaps be clear now, put Ganesh in a very different light—and, along with Ganesh, all the other grotesque figures in the Hindu pantheon, and all the other mythological constructions by which man has tried to come to terms with the intimations of the infinite. And perhaps it is also clearer now what I meant by saying a little while ago that Feuerbach must be stood on his head. To be sure, an elephant-god is a human projection. But an elephant-god is also something else— a symbol of the presence of the infinite within the finitude of the empirical world. One is almost tempted to call it a *projectile*, in this perspective, for the manifestations of the infinite have the character of an invasion, of something thrown onto earth from the heavens in which the gods dwell.

Let me try to sum all this up: If one speaks of religion as a symbol-system, one is referring to two quite different issues. Both are important. Like all human symbolizations, religion refers to the human world—its psychology, its sociology and so forth. Religious symbols stand for human realities. But it is of the very essence of religion that it also has another reference: Religion is an attempt by human beings to symbolize the meta-human, the *other*. Religious symbols, that is, stand for realities that are beyond man and beyond the world of human experience. Unless one understands this dual character of religious symbolization one understands very little about it. There is more: If one does understand this about religion, then one becomes able (hypothetically at the very least) to enter into the peculiar religious view of the human condition. In this view, man himself is a symbol, the empirical world is a symbol—that is, both man and world stand for what is beyond them and what is, at the same time, their ultimate ground. Allow me to put this same proposition in a phrase of my own: Within the empirical world there are signals of transcendence.

Have I fulfilled my assignment here? I'm not sure that I've been witty. I've certainly been theological. Indeed, I have touched upon two issues that, in my opinion, are crucial for the theological enterprise today: the proper understanding of religion as a symbol-system, and the encounter with symbols deriving from religious traditions other than one's own. I cannot be reproached for having had too narrow a focus. If anything, my remarks here have been suffering from a sort of theoretical elephantiasis! The one thing that I haven't done yet is to bring in a Lutheran angle. Let me try.

The obvious Lutheran hook on which to hang my remarks (or perhaps to hang myself) is, of course, the classical proposition that *finitum capax infiniti*. This proposition, if my memory serves me correctly, has its origins in the controversies between Lutherans and Calvinists in the post-Reformation period. I cannot say that these controversies interest me very much. However, I think that this old Lutheran formulation has relevance to the contestation between Christian theology and the reductionist thrust of modern thought.

Human history is full of symbolizations of the infinite. The overwhelming tendency of modern thought has been to reduce these, to translate them, into symbolizations of finitude. In modern thought, the finite is not just capable of the infinite—it swallows it up. The basic proposition of modernity (the essence of modern secularity) is to say: There is nobody here but us humans, each one of us carrying around our little symbol-machine—and sometimes we go a little crazy and fire off our symbols into the sky. This modern proposition is quite correct, as I have argued, but it tells only half the story. For the infinite manifests itself within finitude. When it does, the finite is revealed to be a symbol of the infinite. Even our little symbol-machines are then revealed to be modest, sometimes painfully modest, attempts to imitate the vast symbol that is the cosmos. Furthermore, the manifestations of the infinite within finitude must necessarily appear outlandish, grotesque, absurd. That is, they must appear so to beings such as ourselves, whose organs of perception and modes of expression are geared to the finite world of empirical reality. It is as if two-dimensional beings are trying to cope with a third dimension obtruding into their flat space. Sometimes these obtrusions are so powerful that the human beings who experience them feel that the empirical world has been miraculously transformed. This happens in the experiences that Mircea Eliade has called hierophanies, which the monotheistic traditions of western Asia have subsumed under the category of revelation. For most human beings, however, the presence of the infinite is more veiled, less overpowering. It is encountered within the rituals of tradition and in the signaling experiences of ordinary life. Most of the time, in other words, the infinite is not encountered as a miracle transforming the elements of common reality, but rather "in, with and under" these elements. And among these encounters a very privileged place must be given to the experience of the comic.

Perhaps there has been an involuntarily comic aspect to this presentation, even an unintended joke: It seems that this Lutheran met the Hindu elephant-god . . . Enough. Let me end liturgically: Let us give praise for the elephant!

6 A Funeral in Calcutta*

In India, as in other Third World countries, funerals are a part of ordinary street life in a way they have not been in America for a long time. I once, quite literally, almost ran into one in Calcutta. The procession was upon me suddenly, and I did not realize what it was until I saw the corpse lying openly on a litter covered with flowers. A small group of people were following it out to the *ghat* for the cremation, chanting loudly and, it seemed, fervently. My encounter with the funeral procession was brief, but it was a stark sight, and it impressed itself on my memory. (I saw other funerals later during my stay in India, but this one was the first.) I had been on my way to meet an individual concerned with dialogue between Hindus and Christians, and we talked for a while about funerals. He became eloquent about what he thought to be the beauty of Hindu funerals, and he started to recite, first in Sanskrit, then in English, a passage from

*Theology Today, October 1979

the second chapter of the Bhagavad Gita, customarily chanted on such occasions.

Better hotels in India have not only a Gideon Bible in the rooms but also an English version of the Gita. So, upon returning to my hotel, I looked up the passage. I had read it before, but had not previously known its *Sitz im Leben* in contemporary Hinduism. In Swami Nikhilananda's translation it goes as follows: "Even as a person casts off worn-out clothes and puts on others that are new, so the embodied Self casts off worn-out bodies and enters into others that are new. Weapons cut It not; fire burns It not; water wets It not; the wind does not wither It. This Self cannot be cut nor burnt nor wetted nor withered. Eternal, all-pervading, unchanging, immovable, the Self is the same for ever. This Self is said to be unmanifest, incomprehensible, and unchangeable. Therefore, knowing It to be so, you should not grieve."

The last line, of course, links the metaphysics of the true self with the consolation sought by those mourning this particular body that is about to be burnt. It contains within itself the central theodicy of Hindu faith: "*Therefore*, knowing It to be so, you should not grieve." Raimundo Panikkär, in his monumental work *The Vedic Experience*, translates the line as: "Therefore, recognizing him as such, you should not be distressed." And he elaborates in a footnote: "You should not grieve, mourn, pain, feel sorrow." The fact that the true self is translated as "It" by Nikhilananda and as "he" by Panikkär is, needless to say, not without significance in the context of Hindu theodicy.

Were they consoled, the people walking behind the corpse on the streets of Calcutta? I cannot say; I hope so. But, after reading the passage in my hotel room, I concluded forcefully that I would *not* be consoled. More precisely, even if I gave credence to the metaphysics, I could not accept the "therefore" that is supposed to offer comfort. Why?

As I was reflecting about this, one single word of New Testament Greek occurred to me: *Ephapax* or "once and for all." The word is used several times in Paul's Letter to the Hebrews, referring to the redemptive work of Christ. But it was not its Christological reference that I had in mind at that moment, but rather a much more general reference to what, I suppose, could be described as a specifically Judaeo-Christian sense of life, a sense of the dramatic, decisive meaning of *this* body, *this* life, *this* world. And, of course, it was precisely this sense of life that impelled the Jewish religious tradition toward faith in the resurrection of the dead, a faith that celebrates both physical being and individual particularity.

If my reaction to the Calcutta funeral simply verified the fact that I am a Westerner, with sensibilities formed by centuries of Judaeo-Christian civilization, it would hardly be worth reflecting about. After all, if the modern disciplines of history and the social sciences have taught us anything, it is the relativity of world-views. Discovering myself to be a Westerner in a hotel room in Calcutta might be an interesting personal experience, but it does not raise any new theoretical problems. The matter becomes interesting in a very different way the moment one passes from, broadly speaking, the sociology of knowledge to questions of truth. Let it be stipulated that an individual shaped by a Judaeo-Christian culture perceives the world differently from one brought up as a Hindu and that these different perceptions reach down into the emotional core of personality that is aroused in any serious encounter with death. Let it be further stipulated that the historians and social scientists (and throw in philosophers and psychologists, if you will) can exhaustively explain why this is so, and how it came about. The question still remains, however: Who is right, as between these two ways of "being in the world"? *What is the truth?*

I first traveled to India just after finishing work on my book *The Heretical Imperative*. Appropriately enough, that book ended with the proposition that a great contestation was brewing between the religious traditions emanating from western Asia and those with their roots on the Indian subcontinent. I had proposed also that this contestation, which I described as between the symbolic centers of Jerusalem and Benares, should be of vital concern to Christian theology. Travel was once characterized by someone as a crutch for those deficient in imagination. This may be too harsh a statement, but I'm quite sure that jet-propelling one's organism over the surface of the planet, even with longish stop-overs *en route*, is not a necessary condition of coming to grips with foreign worldviews and traditions. Yet the physical encounter with India seems to have a very specific quality for most people, especially those with religious obsessions. I have such obsessions, for better or for worse, and the encounter certainly had a specific quality for me—one of great intensity.

Many Westerners react to India with revulsion. In most cases, I daresay, this comes from the massive human misery that is all too readily visible in that country. I too was taken aback by some of the things I saw (Calcutta, for one, is as shocking as its reputation), but I had seen equal misery in southeast Asia, in Africa and in Latin America. And whatever one may believe to be the causes and the possible remedies for this misery (as a sociologist I have some ideas about both), it is not plausible to place the blame on the religious traditions of India. Other Westerners, of course, come to India with high expectations of religious and philosophical enlightenment, and even with the expectation of finding some decisive redemptive insight. That was not my case either; I do not expect salvific experiences in out-of-the-way places and I'm not looking for a new faith to be converted to. But the physical encounter with India provided the most intense emotional, existential confirmation of what I had previously believed intellectually: *Here is the most important alternative to the sense of life, religious and otherwise, which has come down to use from the collective experiences of ancient Israel and ancient Greece. And this alternative is not there only as a theoretical possibility. It concerns me existentially, and vitally so. It must be taken with utmost seriousness.*

I summed up this reaction in the first letter I wrote home after arriving in India. I wrote that I had the feeling as if, all along, India had been waiting for me. I would now add: *India is waiting for all of us.* But what does this mean?

It is, of course, fallacious to counterpose the West and India (Jerusalem and Benares, if you will) in neat antithetical categories. In both cases we are dealing with immensely complex and variegated civilizations, and in the course of their long history they have often enough interpenetrated each other. Nevertheless, it is important not to fudge the profound differences in the senses of life, of death and of human destiny that underlie the theodicies of the Gita and of the Judaeo-Christian hope for resurrection. This is certainly not a new discovery. Over and over again, on both sides, it has occasioned what, in the context of the sociology of knowledge, one calls nihilation—that is, theoretical procedures by which an alternative definition of reality is liquidated, superseded, or declared to be null and void. As Hindus and Buddhists are fond of pointing out, the monotheistic religions, notably Christianity and Islam, have a long history of anathematizing alternative modes of religious experience and thought. But the religious traditions of India, Hinduism most of all, have their own strategies of nihilation, more subtle perhaps but thereby no less intolerant—as when Christian or Muslim piety is interpreted as a childish stage in religious evolution.

Nihilation is a fascinating topic for investigation by the historian, phenomenologist or sociologist of religion. It is, I believe, a very sterile exercise for the theologian—and I will include in this designation anyone who seriously reflects on the question of religious truth. I find it very hard indeed to assume that millennia of human experience and thought can be subsumed under the category of error, no matter whether this is done in the harsh terms of Christian or Muslim dogma, or in the all-absorbing embrace of Hindu or Buddhist soteriology. As soon as the nihilating option is rejected, however, an enormously challenging question appears: *If indeed there are highly discrepant experiences between these two worlds, in what manner can both be understood as truth?*

I hasten to add that the last possible answer I have in mind here is some variety of syncretism, a least common denominator, a "soft" theology in which all jagged edges are smoothed over. On the contrary, I'm persuaded that the hard clashes of religious sensibilities must be experienced and reflected upon as clearly as possible—but always in the anticipation of an as yet unimaginable transcendence. This anticipation, of course, is in itself an act of faith. It follows necessarily, I believe, from the conviction that the God we know is a God of truth. It was that same conviction that allowed Christian theology at least twice to risk the fullest possible vulnerability to the critical scrutiny of Greek philosophy, in the patristic age and once again in medieval scholasticism. A comparable conviction made possible the encounter between Christian thought, especially in Protestantism, and the relativizing force of modern philosophical, historical and social-scientific analysis. The contestation with Benares holds risks as great, but also as great a promise.

In a contestation such as this the outcome cannot be known. If it were, the contestation would be fraudulent (like the so-called debates with Jews sometimes staged by Christian authorities in the Middle Ages, with the result firmly fixed in advance). Thus I cannot say how it will be possible to answer the question of truth that is at issue between Jerusalem and Benares. But I do have some idea as to the forms this question will have to take.

The passage from the Gita mentioned before, of course, raises the question of reincarnation. Within Christian theology it has been pretty much shelved since Origen. Is there any way in which the cosmology of *samsara*, be it in some of its Hindu or in its

Buddhist versions, could be incorporated within the Judaeo-Christian experience of creation and human destiny? Then there is once again the question of monotheism and of the particularity of revelation. Must the experience of the oneness of God—the experience of Moses on Sinai and, in its sharpest possible form, of Muhammad on Mount Hira—rigorously exclude all other hierophanies? Put differently, is there nothing to be said, from the standpoint of Jerusalem, about the three hundred thousand gods of Hinduism—except that they are idols? For Christians, the experience of the one God is inextricably intertwined with the figure of Jesus Christ, a figure of scandalous historical particularity. Will it ever be possible to say that God, who was in Jesus Christ, was also incarnate in other figures? Put differently, where are the boundaries of the Logos? This is the question that Raimundo Panikkär has passionately pursued since his early work *The Unknown Christ of Hinduism.* And then there is the question of nature. We know how and why ancient Israel violently rejected the nature cults of the surrounding Near Eastern civilizations, and we may say that this rejection was an inner necessity of Israel's experience of God. But does that necessity still hold? Is it a timeless necessity? As one observes the pilgrims in Benares, streaming with songs and flowers toward the Ganges, one must raise this question: Can we, Jewish and Christian children of Israel, have no part in this experience of the holy river that unites us with the world, with the gods and with all beings? Must we simply say *nein*? Or could it be that the issue between Elijah and the priests of Baal must somehow be reopened, all these many centuries after that violent day on Mount Carmel?

Not far from Benares is Sarnath, where the Buddha began his preaching mission. There is an ancient *stupa* commemorating the event, and on the alleged site of the Deer Park mentioned in the Buddhist scriptures there are several monasteries inhabited by monks from different Asian countries. It is a place of great tranquillity, all the more palpable after the crowded tumultuousness of Benares. For me, it is here that the contestation takes its most pressing form, in a place that arguably expresses the apex of Indian spirituality. Wherever one looks there are Buddhas, in stone or in gold, sitting in the lotus position in timeless repose. The physical posture manifests the religious experience of interiority that, it seems, originated in the oldest civilizations of India—sculptures of men in the lotus position have been excavated at the pre-Aryan sites in the Indus Valley. And, with all due respect for the intermediary forms of religious experience, this interiority stands in sharp antithesis to the confrontational encounters of western Asia—Moses before the burning bush, Paul on the road to Damascus, Muhammad in the night of Qadr. The question could be put this way: As God spoke out of the burning bush, can we imagine Moses sitting in the lotus position? Or could the Lord Buddha, as he sat under the bo tree, have received the Torah? And if both replies are negative, why is this so?

I do not claim necessary priority for this form of the question. It seems to me, however, that in the contestation between interiority and confrontation are contained most of the problems that Judaeo-Christian thought will have to deal with as it meets up with India. The field of comparative mysticism is of crucial importance in this connection; I find the recent work of William Johnston (as in his recent book, *The Inner Eye of Love*, with its provocative comparison of Buddhist *shunyata* and Christian *kenosis*) very helpful in this respect. But that field cannot tackle the problem by itself, because it is precisely the *non*-mystical forms of religious experience that force the contestation. It is also very clear to me that no individual, however learned, can make much headway in this matter alone. What is required are groups of individuals, with different religious commitments and different types of scholarly expertise, coming together around these problems over long periods of time.

* * *

The only time I attended a Protestant worship service during my stay in India was in Bangalore (where I visited the Christian Institute for the Study of Religion and Society, one of the most fruitful places for Hindu-Christian dialogue). The service was in an old Anglican church, now belonging to the Church of South India, close to the military cantonment and right across from a statue of Queen Victoria. All around the church building were plaques commemorating this or that event (mostly deaths) of British army days; I sat near one in memory of a very young army officer, who died (apparently of disease) in the 1920s. The service was in English, in the CSI modification of the Book of Common Prayer. The congregation worshipping in this monument to the British Raj, however, was almost entirely Indian. I was struck by the fact that many people left their shoes behind and walked up barefoot to receive communion, and I reflected that no Western penitential meaning was to be ascribed to this, but rather the more interesting meaning that Indians normally take their shoes off at home. This congregation of Indian Christians felt perfectly at home in this setting, which, to an outsider, seemed like a curious cultural transplant. The shock for me came with the reading of the Gospel: It was the story of Jesus' healing of the centurion's servant.

The shock was sociological rather than theological. It occurred to me just then that here indeed was a gathering of the centurion's servants, long after the centurion's departure, and that this was a poignant way of describing Protestantism in India (not at all, let me hasten to add, a pejorative one). But the same description, in an extended sense, applies to all of Christianity in Asia—an offspring of Western imperialism, now surviving with more or less adaptation in the wake of the imperial era. Christianity has made a deep impact on the consciousness of Asia, both directly in religious form (one must only think of Gandhi here) and indirectly in the form of modernization (which, at its very roots,

131

is a Western and thus Christian phenomenon). What I see on the horizon now is Asia returning the compliment.

Richard Taylor, who is on the staff of the Bangalore Institute, has written a delightful little book entitled *Jesus in Indian Paintings*. I particularly like the pictures of the Moghul school, which testify to the surprising cultural and religious openness of this period in the history of Indian Islam. Here are all the familiar scenes of Christian hagiography—the Holy Family, the Last Supper, the Passion—and in every one of them Jesus looks at us in the figures of Muslim imagination. It is a startling experience of what Brecht called *Verfremdung* in the theater—the familiar made new by being presented in strange forms. What is happening now, perhaps, is a yet more startling manifestation of this process of cross-cultural transformation. The gods and the bodhisattvas of India have begun to appear in Western cities and university campuses, unfamiliar to most of us. Will it be possible for us to recognize a familiar face "in, with and under" these strange figures? Where are the boundaries of the Logos?

7 From Secularity to World Religions*

To be asked to tell how one's mind has changed over a decade is an invitation to narcissism. To accept the invitation would seem to imply a quite solemn view of one's own importance. My incurably Lutheran sensibility tells me that such a view is sinful and my even more incurable sense of the comic that it is ridiculous. Still, after an initial hesitation, I accepted, and did so precisely because I believe that my mind is not so unusual for its peregrinations not to have some common utility. My experiences over the last ten years are, by and large, commonly accessible, and it seems to me that most of my conclusions could be arrived at by anybody.

In 1969 my book *A Rumor of Angels* was published and in 1979 my book *The Heretical Imperative*. In the intervening years, most of my work as a sociologist was not directly concerned with religion, but with modernization and Third World development as well as with the problem, which first preoccupied me in the

The Christian Century, January 16, 1980

Third World, of how sociological insights can be translated into compassionate political strategies. Yet these sociological excursions, as it turned out, had an indirect effect on my thinking about religion.

If I were asked for the most important experience leading from the one book to the other, I would have to say the Third World. In the 1960s I was preoccupied with the problem of secularity, and *A Rumor of Angels* was an attempt to overcome secularity from within. The Third World taught me how ethnocentric that preoccupation was: Secularization is today a worldwide phenomenon, that is true, but it is far more entrenched in North America and in Europe than anywhere else. A more global perspective inevitably provides a more balanced view of the phenomenon. Conversely, the Third World impresses one with the enormous social force of religion. It is this very powerful impression that eventually led me to the conclusion, stated in *The Heretical Imperative*, that a new "contestation" with the other world religions should be a high priority on the agenda of Christian theology.

My own thinking did not move in a radical way during this period. The problems that preoccupied me shifted considerably, but my underlying religious and political positions remained more or less the same. To the extent that I have moved, though, I have moved further to the left theologically and further to the right politically. This has confused and also distressed some of my friends. Again, the Third World has been crucial to both movements of thought. It has given me empirical access to the immense variety and richness of human religion, and thus made it impossible for me—once and for all, I believe—to remain ethnocentrically fixated on the Judaeo-Christian tradition alone. I moved more radically in the 1950s and early 1960s in my thinking about religion (mainly, it seems in retrospect, under the impact of experiencing America after what John Murray Cuddihy has aptly called "the fanaticisms of Europe"), outgrowing the neo-orthodox positions of my youth and finally concluding that my thinking fitted best within the tradition of Protestant liberalism. But the personal as well as intellectual encounter with the Third World gave that liberalism a scope that I could not have foreseen earlier.

I can say with confidence that the human misery of Third World poverty and oppression has shocked me as deeply as it can anyone coming from the comfortable West, and I have been and continue to be convinced of the urgency of seeking alleviation for this misery. But my efforts to understand the causes of this misery and to conceive plausible strategies for overcoming it have impressed upon me the utter fatuity of those alleged solutions advocated by the political left. To be sure, this insight has not in itself been theologically productive, but it has prevented me from taking the currently fashionable route of doing theology by baptizing the empty slogans of this or that version of Marxism with Christian terminology.

The decade staked out by this essay coincides with visits to Rome both at the beginning and the end. In 1969 I organized and chaired a conference there on behalf of the Vatican's Secretariat for Non-Believers. It was a fascinating event, especially in the contacts it provided between members of the Roman ecclesiastical establishment and a somewhat wild assortment of scholars who had worked on the problem of secularization. (The proceedings of the conference were subsequently published in a book aptly entitled *The Culture of Unbelief*.)

One incident from the conference that has stuck in my memory took place at a party. A leading Demochristian politician, very puzzled, asked a monsignor from the Secretariat what this conference was all about. "*La secolarizzazione*," replied the monsignor. "*Secolarizzazione*," repeated the politician, who then asked: "What is this?" The monsignor valiantly rose to the challenge and gave a rather adequate ten-minute summary. The crusty old gentleman of the Democrazia Christiana listened carefully, then raised his hand and said in a firm voice: "We will not permit it!'' At the time, the remark impressed me as very funny. A few weeks later I went to Mexico, at the invitation of Ivan Illich, a trip that turned out to be decisive in concentrating my attention on the Third World. I remember telling Illich the story. He laughed but he did not think it as funny as I did. Illich is often right (often, not always). In this instance, his finding the idea of prohibiting secularization less outrageous than I found it was wise.

In 1979 I was in Rome just as the Iranian revolution was breaking out. I watched the events in Iran on Italian television with a good deal of nervousness, as I was supposed to fly to India via Tehran. There were the vast masses of Khomeini followers, with their posters and banners, seemingly stretching to the horizon. And they kept chanting *"Allahu l'akbar!"*—"God is great!'' I thought of that remark about secularization of a decade ago, and it did not seem funny at all. Indeed, a dramatic prohibition of secularization is exactly what Khomeini had in mind, and, whatever the eventual outcome of the Iranian revolution, it must be conceded that he was rather successful in this undertaking. Certainly in the Islamic world, from the Atlantic Ocean to the China Sea, it is religion that offers a militant challenge to every form of secularity (including the Marxist one), and not the other way around.

In any event, the turmoil in Iran forced me to change my travel plans and fly directly to India. This was my first visit there and one that immersed me more completely than ever before in a non-Western religious culture. And while Hinduism, for many reasons, does not exhibit the dynamism of contemporary Islam, it most assuredly is not behaving as the idea of secularization I held in the 1960s would predict.

My encounter with the Third World is not the only reason why I have modified my earlier view of secularization. There has been impressive evidence of religious resurgence in North America. There has also been the significant religious revival in at least certain sectors of Soviet society, all the more significant because of a half century of determined and sophisticated repression. This does not mean, as some have suggested, that the secularization theory has been simply a mistake. But one can now say, I think, that both the extent and the inexorability of secularization have been exaggerated, even in Europe and North America, much more so in other parts of the world. In itself, this is no more than a revision of a sociological thesis under the pressure of empirical evidence. As such, it is theologically neutral. Yet, inevitably, it suggests that the problem of secularity is not quite as interesting for the Christian mind as many of us used to think. After all, it is one thing to engage in intellectual contestation with a phenomenon deemed to be the wave of the future, quite another to do so with one of the many cultural currents presently in play in the contemporary world.

Sociologically speaking, the phenomenon of secularization is part and parcel of a much broader process—that of modernization. In the context of Christian theology, of course, the dialogue with secularity (or the mind-set resulting from secularization) has been pretty much the same as the dialogue with modernity, or with that well-known figure "modern man," whom Rudolf Bultmann and others conceived to be incapable of believing the worldview of the New Testament. Speaking sociologically again, there are good reasons for thinking that modernity, and modern secularity with it, are in a certain crisis today. It became clear to me in the Third World that modernization is not a unilinear or inexorable process. Rather, from the beginning, it is a process in ongoing interaction with countervailing forces, which may be subsumed under the heading of counter-modernization. It is useful, I think, to look at secularization in the same way—as standing in ongoing interaction with counter-secularizing forces. Without exploring all the details of this interaction, suffice it to say that counter-modernization and counter-secularization can be observed not only in the Third World but also in the so-called advanced industrial societies, both those of the capitalist and of the socialist varieties.

All of this strongly suggests a shift in theological attention, away from the much-vaunted engagement with modern consciousness and its theoretical products. It should be stressed that this is not to say that some of the latter products do not continue to offer theological challenges. I suspect that this is particularly true of developments in the physical sciences, those prime products of modernity. It is also apparent that theories and worldviews apart, the modern situation continues to pose ethical problems of great gravity—but that is not quite the same as what the dialogue with ''modern man'' was to be about. I would also like it to be clear that in saying modern consciousness is not as interesting theologically as many have thought (or not as interesting as it once was—for example in the nineteenth century, when Christian theology had to deal with the challenge of modern historical thought), I'm not in the least implying some sort of anti-modern stance. There is much of this around today (for instance, in the more radical stance of the ecology movement), and some of it is quite appealing, but it will not stand up under rigorous scrutiny. It is not so much that we cannot go back (there is no law that says that the clock cannot be turned back—it can be, it has), but that the human costs of demodernizing would be horrendously large.

Already in the early 1960s, when I was working with Thomas Luckmann on new ways of formulating the sociology of knowledge, it had become clear to us that secularization and pluralism were closely related phenomena. The root insight here is that subjective certainty—in religion as in other matters—depends upon cohesive social support for whatever it is that the individual wants to be certain about. Conversely, the absence or weakness of social support undermines subjective certainty—and that is precisely what happens when the individual is confronted with a plurality of competing competing worldviews, norms or definitions of reality. I continue to think that this insight is valid. Increasingly, though, it has seemed to me that of the two phenomena, pluralism is more important than secularization. Put differently: The modern situation would present a formidable challenge to religion even if it were, or would come to be, much less secularized than it now is.

Competition means having to choose. This is true in a market of material commodities—this brand against that, this consumer option against that. Whether one likes this or not, the same compulsion to choose is the result of a market of worldviews—this faith, or this "lifestyle," against another. I have called this crucial consequence of pluralism "the heretical imperative," and I have tried in my book of that title to analyze different theological responses to this rather uncomfortable situation. Again, I do not perceive my thinking as having changed dramatically on these matters. But at least two accents have changed. First, it is much clearer to me now why the theological method (not necessarily any of the contents) of classical Protestant liberalism, with its stress on experience and reasonable choice, is the most viable one today. And two, because of my previously mentioned encounter with the Third World, I now have a much broader notion of the range of relevant choices in religion.

As a result of this perspective on the religious situation and its theological possibilities, I have for quite a while found myself in a sort of two-front position. Confronting the theological right, I'm convinced that any attempts to reconstruct old certainties, as if "the heretical imperative" could be ignored, are futile. This conviction makes it impossible for me to seek alignment with any form of orthodoxy or neo-orthodoxy. On the other hand, I see no more promise in the left's strategies of trying to make Christianity plausible by secularizing its contents, no matter whether this "secularization from within" (one of Luckmann's helpful terms) is done by means of philosophy, psychology or political ideology. All these strategies are finally self-liquidating, as they rob the religious enterprise of whatever plausibility it still has within the consciousness of individuals. Incidentally, this does not mean that I have no empathy with either the right or the secularizing left's positions. The former was the position of my youth, in the form of a sort of muscular Lutheranism, and, if nothing else, the nostalgia of middle age assures a lingering empathy. As to the latter position, it is not just a matter of "some of my best friends" and all that, but an empathetic recognition that anyone who lives and works in a modern secular milieu faces every day the same cognitive tensions that move people toward this position.

With regard to this, a word should be said about an event with which I was associated, the so-called Hartford Appeal of 1975. This was a statement that forcefully repudiated various secularizing trends in contemporary theological thought. It was widely understood as a neo-orthodox manifesto. Whatever may have been the understanding of others connected with the event, this was not the way I understood it. For me, Hartford delineated what separated me from those to the left of the liberal position I espoused. I do believe that such delineation continues to be necessary, though, in retrospect, it is debatable whether the style of the Hartford Appeal was the most suitable. For me, however, delineation with regard to the theological right is equally important, and I hope that *The Heretical Imperative* has fulfilled this purpose.

The worst thing about being in the middle is not that one is shot at from both sides. In this instance that is not so bad, as there are a lot of people in the same location. More disturbing is the thought that a *via media*, especially in religion, is always beset with tepidness. And that has indeed been one of the recurring qualities of Protestant liberalism. True enough, but I don't think that this is a necessary quality. Every nuanced, reflected-upon position is in danger of appearing tepid in comparison with the self-confident postures of those who claim certainty. It is important to understand the illusionary character of the self-confident postures, at which point mellowness acquires its own certainty, more quiet perhaps than that of the Barthians, say, or Christian revolutionaries, but also more enduring.

Speaking of Barthians, there is one question that concerned them from the beginning, indeed that first motivated Karl Barth himself in his early theological thinking: "How does one preach that?" The question is a crucial one, not only for those who are vocationally charged with preaching, but also for those (including myself) who are committed to the public reaffirmation of the Christian tradition. It is many years now since, after one very happy year at the Lutheran Theological Seminary in Philadelphia, I drew back from the ministry as my own vocational goal. All biographical decisions are murky, but this one was essentially simple: I felt that I could not be a Lutheran minister unless I could fully assent to the definition of the faith as stated in the Lutheran confessions, and I drew back from this role because I doubted whether I could give such unqualified assent. In other words, I felt that I, for one, could not preach "that." I do not regret this long-ago decision, but it is relevant to these observations that today I would arrive at a different conclusion. If "that" is now understood as being the liberal position alluded to above, then I'm deeply convinced that it can indeed be preached—and, given the cell to do that, I'm convinced that I could.

The reason for this conclusion is also essentially simple: I believe that at the core of the Christian tradition is truth, and this truth will reassert itself in every conceivable contestation, be it with the multiform manifestations of modern secularity, or with the powerful traditions of Asian religion awaiting theological engagement. To be sure, no one who honestly enters into such a contestation emerges the way he entered; if he did, the contestation was probably less than honest. In the act of reflection, every honest individual must be totally open, and this also means open-ended. The act of preaching is different. Here the individual does not stand before the tradition in the attitude of reflection but deliberately enters into that tradition and reaffirms the truth that he has discovered through it, without thereby forgetting or falsifying the fruits of reflection.

There is no way of predicting the movements of the spirit. I have often thought that a person equipped with all the tools of modern social science would have been hard put to predict the Reformation, say, at the onset of the sixteenth century. I will not make a prediction here, but I will make a guarded statement: It is possible that out of the contestations of our time will emerge preaching voices of great and renewed power. There is a kind of stillness now, and has been for quite some time. It is possible that the stillness will be followed by thunder. We do not know this. We are not supposed to know. But the possibility is worth a cautious hope, and perhaps even a gamble of faith.

8 Moral Judgment and Political Action*

The topic I have chosen to address in this lecture is age-old. It has been pondered over for centuries by sages and lesser minds in all the great civilizations. It is, in the final analysis, the relation of power and virtue, *kratos* and *areté*. Not exactly a narrow, circumscribed topic! You have every right to be skeptical as to whether I will have anything original to contribute, and you may also anticipate that having mustered the chutzpah of addressing this topic, I will deservedly make a fool of myself in the attempt. So it may turn out. But I do want to say at the outset that it is not my intention to announce the discovery of some new points of political ethics that were lamentably overlooked by Plato, Aristotle, St. Augustine, or Confucius. Whatever other vices I may have developed, any tendency toward megalomania has been severely crippled in my case by a seemingly ineradicable sense of the ridiculous. My intention here is more modest. It

*Lecture, Boston University, October 1987, published in *This World*, Spring 1988

is to report on some insights that I think I have gained over the years in trying to relate my own intellectual discipline, that of sociology, to the political challenges we face in the modern world as citizens of a democracy. Put differently, my attempt here is to show how a social-scientific perspective may be useful to anyone who seeks to act politically in a morally responsible way.

The phrase "in the modern world" should be stressed. While power and virtue have been in tension ever since human beings began to reflect about their condition, there are some new aspects to this tension in the modern period. There is the institutional fact of the modern state, a *novum* in history because of the unprecedented concentration of power it represents. There is also a fact in the realm of human consciousness, namely the relativization of beliefs and values, which, as I have tried to demonstrate in much of my work in the sociology of knowledge, is endemic to the modern situation. These two facts, taken together, have resulted in a very peculiar reformulation of the old tension. On the one hand, there is the rise of *raison d'état*, that very distinctive, though not unique, Western tradition of political thought, classically described in Friedrich Meinecke's great work *Die Idee der Staatsräson* (regrettably and very misleadingly titled *Machiavellism* in the English translation). Paradoxically, the modern period has also engendered the rise of miscellaneous political utopias and soteriologies, which passionately repudiate not only the validity but even the fact of *raison d'état*. We thus find ourselves beset by a strange interplay of contradictory ideas, embodied in psychologically contrary human types—coolly pragmatic rationality poised against quasi-religious faiths, in the extreme cases embodied, respectively, in heartless technocrats locked in political battles with mindless ideologues. A morally unattractive choice. I would contend that if a social-scientific perspective does nothing else than suggest a more palatable option, it will have justified itself as an intellectual enterprise.

It is now almost seventy years ago that Max Weber delivered his famous lecture "Politics as a Vocation" at the University of Munich. The moment was dramatic—one year after Germany's catastrophic defeat in World War I, in the city that was the epicenter of revolutionary turmoil both of the left and the right, with an audience of students many of whom were veterans of the war, bearing its physical and psychic scars. In this lecture, of course, Weber among other things made the distinction between two types of ethics that he called *Gesinnungsethik* and *Verantwortungsethik*, roughly translatable as an "ethic of attitude" and an "ethic of responsibility." Much of the lecture consists of Weber's eloquent advocacy of the latter. It is a measure of Weber's stature that despite all the differences between that moment in history and our own, his argument is uncannily, even urgently, relevant to anyone who today wants to act politically in a morally defensible manner.

Gesinnungsethik is the view that what matters morally is the attitude of the actor; if that attitude is morally pure, then the actions following from it are morally valid. *Gesinnungsethik* has also been more freely translated as an "ethic of absolute ends": If the ends of action are morally unexceptional, then the actor can leave aside the weighing of means and consequences. The extreme form of this ethical stance is well expressed in the Roman adage "*fiat iustitia pereat mundus*"—"let justice be done, let the world perish." It is worth noting that while firmly rejecting this moral stance, Weber had a good deal of respect for it. For him, such an ethic was typified by the pacifism of Tolstoy, a man he greatly admired (an admiration, I must say, which I don't share). Be this as it may, let me say that I too would not altogether repudiate this moral stance in certain instances. For example, I'm unalterably, passionately (if you like, dogmatically) opposed to capital punishment. My reason for this is my conviction that capital punishment is an act of such monstrous cruelty that it ought not to be in the arsenal of legal sanctions of a civilized society. Indeed, I believe that its very existence, its presence in the legal code and its use by the authorities, constitutes *ipso facto* a morally grave indictment of the society that allows it (as, alas, is the case with the United States today). Now, holding this moral belief and the attitude (*Gesinnung*) that goes with it, I'm not really interested (at least not morally interested) in the debate as to whether capital punishment does or does not deter certain crimes such as murder. As far as I can judge, those who argue that it does not deter have the better evidence. But if the weight of evidence should shift to the other side, I would not be shaken in my position. I'm well aware of the fact that in this position I stand with a minority of Americans (and, incidentally, it is a position that divides me from most of my conservative friends). For all I know, many of you advocate the death penalty for reasons that make sense to you. So let me take another example, which, I daresay, almost all of us would agree on in America today: Even if criminologists could demonstrate that torturing suspects reduces the murder rate, we would not therefore favor its reintroduction into police procedure.

Yet even here, where a moral belief is absolute and *ipso facto* meta-political, *I* must weigh means and probable consequences if I want to act politically in order to abolish capital punishment. I would not, say, advocate assaulting judges who impose the death penalty, or take this issue as the only one by which a candidate for office is to be judged, or work toward the destruction of the entire American legal system because it tolerates this barbarity. And my reasons for not recommending or embarking upon such courses of action are, of course, based on an assessment of consequences as well as chances of success. With such an assessment, I already step into the realm of an "ethic of responsibility." In other words, as soon as I want to achieve empirical results by my actions, I must entertain considerations other than those dictated by my moral absolutes. I step, if you will, into the realm of political logic, which allows few if any absolutes.

Weber was right in his central proposition: Whatever the ultimate source or status of our moral beliefs, when we seek to be politically effective, we can only operate with an "ethic of responsibility." What we must then do is calculate the appropriateness of available means to desired ends, to look at the probabilities of success, to attempt to foresee both intended and unintended consequences. Needless to say, we now step from a world of moral certainties to a world of uncertainty, relativity and compromise. This latter world, of course, is the world of the empirical—the messy, confusing, often deadly reality of human history. There are no guarantees in this world. It is precisely at this point that the social sciences come in; they are, after all, concerned with illuminating this empirical reality of human actions. In what follows all I propose to do is to suggest four intellectual contributions that the social sciences can make toward morally responsible action in the political arena.

The first contribution is *the discipline of detachment*. In recent years there has been endless discussion in the social sciences about what Weber called "value-freeness"—that is, about the question whether the social sciences can or should be morally neutral. Most of this discussion has been an unoriginal and rather dreary repetition of arguments made more interestingly in Weber's time. I will not go into this in any great detail. At the risk of simplification, however, I will point out that the quarrel has been between two groups—on one side, positivists who maintain that facts in the human sciences are just like facts in the natural sciences, and on the other side, theorists (interestingly both on the left and the right, such as Marxists and Straussians) who insist that all human facts are subject to interpretation and therefore inaccessible to morally neutral analysis. Both groups, I think, are partially right but finally mistaken (and I also think, by the way, that Weber is still the best guide through this methodological minefield). Human society is constituted by meanings and therefore there are, indeed, no "naked facts" over and beyond interpretation. The positivists are wrong when they think that one can do sociology in the way one does zoology: The human beings studied by the sociologist give meaning to their existence, the insects studied by the zoologist (as far as we know) do not, and this difference has far-reaching methodological implications for the two sciences. But when the sociologist tries to understand human beings, it is *their* meanings that he must try to understand, and he cannot do this when he imposes his own. It is this, no more but also no less, that Weber intended by his concept of "value-freeness." Both Marxists and the disciples of Leo Strauss are wrong in thinking that this cannot be achieved.

Ideologies of all political colorations have sought to enlist the human sciences as "weapons" in the war of ideas. The late Dr. Goebbels put it very clearly: "Truth is what serves the German people." Such use of any science destroys its essential character as a disinterested quest for truth. The social scientist has no special qualification as a moralist; his qualification, if any, lies in his trained capacity to assess empirical evidence. Part and parcel of this training is the discipline of detachment, that is, an ability to look at a situation clearly, to bracket one's own feelings and convictions in the effort to understand what others feel and believe, to listen rather than preach. Most important is his ability to look at *reality* even if what comes into view is very much different from what one would wish to be there. This discipline of detachment, of course, is a circumscribed, artificial act. It should not, and indeed cannot, be carried over into the rest of the social scientist's life. Yet, even though limited to specific acts of understanding, it constitutes no mean moral achievement—the capacity to control passion without in any way abandoning it, to cultivate the calm look, to have respect for the real. In this, I would contend, the modern social scientist stands in a great philosophical tradition of what the Greeks called the "theoretical life" (*biòs theoretikcós*). It always seems strange to me that there are people who find greater moral attractiveness in the role of the propagandist.

Let me cite an example from recent American sociology. A few years ago Kristin Luker published a book entitled *Abortion and the Politics of Motherhood*. Luker interviewed two groups of women in California, pro-choice and pro-life activists. Her findings threw original and interesting light on the social characteristics of these two groups. Luker also tried to draw a portrait of the two worldviews at issue, brilliantly so, I thought. This is why I reviewed her book, although this particular topic has never been one on which I have worked myself as a sociologist. I thought that this book, quite apart from the intrinsic significance of its empirical findings, was an excellent illustration of the sociology of knowledge applied to a concrete social phenomenon. What impressed me particularly, and I said so in my review, was that one could read the book from one end to the other without finding out how Luker herself stood on this issue. In other words, to a remarkable degree she showed her discipline of detachment. There is an ironic and, to me, depressing sequel. I was told later that Luker is a committed feminist with strong pro-choice views. This much neither surprised nor depressed me: It is sociologically unlikely that a sociologist holds pro-life views, and my own views in this matter are just about equidistant from the two groups of activists studied by Luker. But what I was also told later (by hearsay) is that Luker subsequently expressed regret that she had not avowed her strong commitment to pro-choice views in her book. In other words, if this account is correct, she confessed as a vice the very detachment that I saw as a major virtue in her book. Whatever may be the facts in this particular case, there is a lot of confusion about morality and methodology in current sociology, and the confusion undercuts the very contribution that sociologists are qualified to make to public debate.

The second contribution is *the clarification of normative and cognitive presuppositions*. In everyday life we constantly employ both kinds of presuppositions: Norms tell us what the world ought to be and how we ought to act; but these norms are supposed to maintain in a world that is real, and we hold a large number of assumptions, or cognitive presuppositions, as to what that reality is. It is important to understand that norms have little if any meaning without the cognitive presuppositions that go with them. For example, anthropologists tell us that one of the most ancient human norms is the incest tabu. This norm tells me that I must not have sexual relations with a close relative. Fine. But who are my "close relatives"? Thus in a particular culture the general norm translates itself into a very specific injunction: "You may not marry your fifth cousin!" I wonder how many of us in this room have the foggiest notion of what a fifth cousin is, let alone which individuals fall into this solemnly proscribed category of people. In other words, we simply (and perhaps to our great loss) lack the cognitive presupposition that would give practical meaning to this norm. A good anthropologist can, of course, tell us why. That is, anthropology as an interpretive human science can draw a "cognitive map" of modern American culture, duly note the absence of these kinship categories from it, and thus explain why the utterance of moral anathemas against those who marry fifth cousins leaves contemporary Americans puzzled and definitely not overwhelmed by pangs of guilt. *Mutatis mutandis*, this dependence of norms on a set of cognitive assumptions holds generally. You may substitute for the incest tabu, as it were, the moral imperative of your choice.

Now, there are cases in which norms directly clash. In that case, the social sciences can clarify the clash but they can do nothing to resolve it. For example, during my military service in the 1950s I was stationed in the Deep South. This was my first personal experience of the system of racial segregation, and it shocked me profoundly. Being a newly minted sociologist, I did a good deal of reading about this matter. I recall a conversation with a very intelligent and well-read white Southerner, a fellow draftee, to whom I communicated all my newly acquired knowledge about race relations—that the notion of race as established in the South was a myth, how that myth served to legitimate a system of oppression and exploitation, and so on. To my surprise, my interlocutor agreed with everything I said: Yes, race was a myth; yes, the myth justified the power and privilege of whites; and so on. Well, I then asked him, how is it that you are not morally troubled by this state of affairs? He shrugged his shoulders and said: "I do very well under this system, and I see no reason why I should feel or do anything that is against my own interests." That was not the end of the conversation, but I realized sharply that no additional amount of empirical evidence could help to dissuade him from a position that I found morally repugnant; the conversation had to move to a different plane, one of ethical and philosophical discourse. (This individual subsequently underwent a sort of moral conversion, but it was certainly not occasioned by new sociological insights—as always, it was a movement within what Pascal called "*la raison du coeur*," that reason of the heart that is very far removed from the rationality of scientific induction.)

At least as common, however, are cases in which sharp disagreements occur between people who have no normative differences in the abstract, but whose divergent cognitive presuppositions lead them to diametrically opposed political and moral conclusions as these norms are concretely applied. Let me take an example here from the area in which I have done most of my work as a sociologist for the last twenty years, the area of Third World development. Over the years I have had many discussions with proponents of Liberation Theology, in Latin America and elsewhere. One of the best-known phrases coming out of this movement is "the preferential option for the poor." There are some nuanced differences in the way this phrase has been used by different authors, but the underlying moral proposition is very clear: The condition of the poor should be the yardstick by which we judge both a society and any projects for changing it. In context, of course, this proposition is further undergirded by reference to the New Testament and a long tradition of Christian ethics. Now, I have no problem whatever with this proposition. It is perfectly plausible to me both ethically and theologically. My profound difficulties with most Liberation Theologians lie not at all in the normative sphere; rather I have great difficulties with their cognitive presuppositions. These, of course, are mostly taken, lock, stock and barrel, from the neo-Marxist theory of Third World underdevelopment. Thus most Liberation Theologians believe that Third World underdevelopment is caused by capitalism; that the Third World is poor because the First World is rich—that is, our wealth depends on their poverty; and, most important in terms of political implication, that socialism is the way out of Third World poverty. It is my opinion, based not on some ethical theorizing but on the reading of the evidence, that every one of these beliefs is empirically false. And, because this is my understanding of the empirical realities, I believe that the socialist strategies recommended by most of these authors are politically disastrous and morally irresponsible—precisely because they will in all likelihood lead to more poverty, more oppression, more exploitation.

I have just completed a two-year stint as chairman of an international study group on the future of South Africa. The agenda of this study was to draw as accurately as possible the ''cognitive maps'' of all the principal actors in the South African drama and to analyze the ''strategic logic'' employed by these actors as they try to move the country from the status quo to a desired future. We could only do this job by agreeing that we would not make any recommendations to anyone. We could not have decided otherwise, since our group contained individuals, both white and black, that ranged (in South African terms) from moderate right to pretty far left; we could never have agreed on any set of political policies. More important, though, there would have been no reason why anyone should be particularly interested in our moral principles or political agendas—both were thoroughly unoriginal. Our contribution, if there was to be one, could only come through an exercise of very cool, detached description and analysis. This has been borne out by the reiterated experience of talking about our findings with people across the political spectrum: Invariably, our interlocutors are most interested in what we have to say about the "cognitive map" and the "strategic logic" of their opponents.

We worked by assigning different actors to different members of the group. Thus the study of the Afrikaner right wing was undertaken by Helen Zille, an Afrikaans-speaking white who is politically on the left and who has a long history of anti-apartheid activity. She produced one of the best papers of the project, a crystal-clear depiction of what this group of actors believes about the world both normatively and cognitively, and of the strategies by which they seek to attain their ends. It was by no means easy for her to do this; she was studying a reality that she detests. But, although she frequently professed her rejection of the idea of "value-free" analysis, she nevertheless, brilliantly if somewhat ironically, produced one of the best examples of this kind of analysis within the project. What is more, only because of this will her part of the final report be useful to those with whom she identifies politically, those who are on the left in the resistance to apartheid.

The image of the mapmaker is heuristically useful. The social scientist, *au fond*, is a maker of maps. If you want to travel from point X to point Y, a map will be useful to you. It can tell you a lot about the territory you must traverse. But it can tell you nothing about the purpose of your journey, or whether you should undertake it in the first place. And the map will be equally useful to you only if it can be equally useful to someone who undertakes the journey for very different, possibly antagonistic purposes.

The mapmaker has no qualifications to advise you about the moral status of your intended journey. The map, of necessity, is morally neutral. But, of course, this does not mean at all that the mapmaker, as a human being, has no moral responsibilities. He may decide that the purpose of your journey is so odious, morally, that he will try to withhold the map from you. It is beyond the scope of this lecture to discuss the moral possibility that in certain cases, a mapmaker may decide to draw a deliberately inaccurate map so as to mislead a putatively odious traveler. It should be quite clear, though, that whatever it is that a mapmaker is doing when he consciously distorts reality for moral reasons, it is *not* social science!

The third contribution is *the social location of actors and their interests*. Much of the output of the human sciences over the last two centuries or so can aptly be subsumed under Nietzsche's category of the "art of mistrust." Historians have asked who really wrote this or that text, psychologists have tried to unmask people's real motives, and so on. The contribution of sociology (and especially of the subdiscipline known as the sociology of knowledge) has been to locate actors and their ideas within society, and in the same process to uncover their vested interests. Put differently, the sociologist is the character who, when confronted with any statement of belief or value, will invariably ask the prototypically mistrustful question, "Says who?" This question, disagreeable though it sounds, is of great importance in clarifying any situation in society and especially any situation within which one intends to act politically. Suppose that one encounters a movement that pushes the idea that the consumption of bananas causes leprosy. Its propaganda, of course, will contain alleged scientific evidence on the leprotic effects of bananas. It will not surprise one that this evidence is vigorously disputed by the association of banana growers. If one is a sociologist, one will be only slightly surprised to discover that the anti-banana movement is sponsored by the league of mango producers (since an economist friend has provided the information that bananas and mangos are in stiff competition on the fruit market). In other words, the sociologist will always look for vested interests, and most of the time the search is successful. It is important to understand that this disclosure of the vested interests in play does not settle the medical question as to whether bananas do or do not cause leprosy. But it is a useful starting point to know about the two sets of vested interests in order to understand the debate, and especially so if one has a political involvement in the issue (say, one is a legislator pondering a bill banning banana advertising).

I have had an intermittent interest over the years in the anti-smoking movement (my original interest sprang from a smoker's annoyance at a rhetoric and at tactics that resembled the excesses of the Salem witch-hunt). Now, the anti-smoking movement continuously inveighs against what it calls the "smoking interests," namely, the tobacco interests and its allies in government. Of course the movement marshals putatively scientific evidence to advance its cause, and of course the tobacco industry has been questioning this evidence. There are indeed "smoking interests." Talk to any legislator from, say, North Carolina. What should not have surprised me but did was the discovery that there are also *anti*-smoking interests—an international consortium of health activists and bureaucrats, who have an enormous stake (in terms of money, power and status) in the success of the movement. And the approach to and use of the evidence by this consortium is as *interested* (that is, biased and, when necessary, selective) as anything evinced by the other side in the debate. Needless to say, this sociological discovery in no way answers the question whether smoking does or does not cause all the diseases now listed on our cigarette packages. (In case you wonder, let me give you my considered opinion that it is indeed better for your health not to smoke—at least not to smoke cigarettes.) But an intriguing question now emerges: The scientific evidence on this issue is exceedingly complicated; most of it is based on sophisticated statistics. Very few people are competent to form an independent opinion. This means that their position, if any, is based on faith in this or that authority. In recent years, in the United States, this has meant faith in statements by the Surgeon General, the head of an agency of the federal government. Now ask yourself why people who will not believe one word pronounced by, say, the Secretary of State (let alone the National Security Adviser) believe that a matter is closed because the Surgeon General says so. It is a sociologically fruitful question to ask!

There is a considerable tradition in modern social thought, going back to Nietzsche, Marx and even before, seeking to expose the relation between ideas and interests. An important question has been whether there are any ideas that are or can be held in a disinterested way (compare, for example, the well-known discussion of this question in Karl Mannheim's book *Ideology and Utopia*). I believe there are. But it is a good rule, whenever any individual or group propounds an alleged truth, to ask whether these people have anything to gain from the allegation. One cannot always answer yes; more often than not one can. This may be, so to speak, philosophically depressing. It remains a crucial fact to keep in mind if one decides to look at the world as it is rather than as one would like it to be.

Let me go back to Kristin Luker's work on abortion in California. The most striking finding coming out of her research was that the two groups of activists, pro-choice and pro-life, were amazingly polarized in terms of occupation and education—in sociological parlance, in terms of *class*. Luker's findings have been supported by other research. It seems that the principal factor determining an individual's (male or female) attitude toward abortion is class—more so even than religion. What this means is very simple. The higher up one goes in the American class system, the more one finds people with pro-abortion attitudes. Why should this be so? Luker's data (which only deal with women, but we know through other studies that men follow the same pattern) give a clear answer: Motherhood is a principal social asset for working-class and lower-middle-class women, while it is a social liability for upper-middle-class women, especially (as is increasingly the case) if the latter are in professional or managerial occupations. In other words, whatever may be the ethical and philosophical aspects of this issue, the way in which people come out on it is very much linked to vested interests, on both sides.

What is even more intriguing is that attitudes toward abortion are embedded in much larger constellations of beliefs and values which are also class-driven. In this connection let me mention what I consider to be one of the most fruitful hypotheses in recent American social science, that of the so-called "New Class." I prefer the term "knowledge class." The hypothesis proposes that there has been a split in what used to be a unified middle class. Where previously there was one, there are now two middle classes. One is the old middle class, derived from the historic bourgeoisie and still centered in the business community. The other is a class constituted by those who derive their livelihood and their status from the production and distribution of knowledge (especially symbolic knowledge, that is, knowledge unrelated to material goods or services). The hypothesis not only affirms that this new knowledge exists (that would be a simple matter of classification) but that it has specific characteristics in terms of worldview and lifestyle. There is now considerable empirical support for this hypothesis. (I cannot resist the temptation of mentioning that one of the first research projects undertaken by the Institute for the Study of Economic Culture at Boston University, which it has been my pleasure to direct, has been an attempt to verify this hypothesis. John McAdams, a political scientist, has re-analyzed a large body of survey data allowing correlations between occupation and a variety of opinions, attitudes and behavior patterns. McAdams' findings strongly support the hypothesis.) The evidence shows that, broadly speaking, the new knowledge class is to the left politically of the old middle class. Why should this be so?

Again, an analysis of vested interests helps us to understand what otherwise would be quite puzzling. In Western democracies, by and large, to be on the left now rarely means embracing a socialist agenda. Rather, the ongoing debate between left and right concerns the scope and nature of government intervention in both the economy and social life. More specifically, the left favors the maintenance and extension of the machinery of the welfare state, while the right is suspicious of it and seeks to limit it. Once one looks at this debate in terms of class interests, all mystery disappears. For the business community the welfare state is, in the main, a liability. The new knowledge class, on the other hand, depends heavily on government subsidization and indeed many of its members are employed in welfare-state bureaucracies. Put differently, much of the current left/right debate is between those who have a vested interest in production and those with an interest in redistribution. Now, it cannot be emphasized strongly enough that such an insight does not, and cannot, resolve any single question raised in the debate, or directly lead to a moral judgment. I may understand that the business class has an interest in lower taxes and the knowledge class in tax-funded policies of redistribution, and I might still decide that morality supports a position favorable to either interest. But I would contend that such an exercise in sociological debunking actually facilitates a clear moral decision: People, of course, always claim that *the other fellow* has vested interests; one's own position, by contrast, is motivated by pure love of humankind or by a disinterested search for truth. This claim, subjected to social-scientific scrutiny, almost never stands up. But this liberates rather than cripples moral judgment. One now understands that there are vested interests all around any given issue, and this understanding gives one a better chance to make a moral judgment on the merits of the case. And one more observation of some usefulness: Once one grasps the power of vested interests in shaping human beliefs and values, one will pay very special attention to moral judgments that appear to be *contrary* to the vested interests of those making them!

Finally, the fourth contribution—*the assessment of tradeoffs*. Milton Friedman is credited with the statement that the most important lesson of economics is that there are no free lunches. Not only economics: The application of all social-scientific perspectives to the realm of moral judgment and political action yields the same lesson. It is the easiest thing in the world to proclaim a good. The hard part is to think through ways by which this good can be realized without exorbitant costs and without consequences that negate the good. That is why an ethic of responsibility must be cautious, calculating a perennially uncertain mass of means, costs and consequences. This is tedious and endlessly frustrating, which is why so many people, especially young people, are drawn to an ethic of attitude: *Moral purity is one of the cheapest human achievements*. Its results can usually be summed up in this or that paraphrase of the famous statement by an American officer during the Vietnam war: "We had to destroy the village in order to liberate it."

Let me speak about Vietnam for a few moments, and do so in a slightly confessional tone (this may be acceptable in a lecture dealing with moral judgment). In the late 1960s I was actively involved with the anti-war movement. I was not on the left then any more than I'm now. I was part of that segment of the anti-war movement (probably its majority) which had no particular admiration for the other side in that conflict and which was simply motivated by revulsion against the inhumanities perpetrated by our side. Our motives, in retrospect, were, if not pure, quite unexceptionable. Here were atrocious acts committed by the United States and its allies. We felt responsible as American citizens, and therefore saw it as our responsibility to act politically in order to stop the war. We were successful beyond our wildest dreams. We did stop the war. We did not do this by ourselves, of course (the anti-war movement at home was not the only reason why the United States quit Indochina), but we certainly contributed in a significant way. As political actions go, we were indeed successful: We did nothing less than help bring about the first abject defeat in the history of the United States.

This episode in my political biography (such as it is) has taught me a number of very important lessons. Some are not relevant to the present topic (such as lessons about alliances with the ideological left or about trusting the American media for information). But the most important lesson has been one which, at that stage of my life, I should really not have had to learn: When it comes to politics, we get no moral brownie points for good intentions; we will be judged by the results. And the results of these particular political actions have been massive and almost all bad. Let me leave aside results that are still to be seen in American domestic politics and in the international system, mostly bad ones. Instead let me just mention the results for the people of Indochina, those people in sympathy with whom our actions were undertaken in the first place. In South Vietnam the result was the imposition of a relentless totalitarian tyranny, which not only led to political oppression vastly worse than that practiced by the dictatorship with which the United States was allied during the war, but which also afflicted the country with demented economic policies that have made it a basket case of Southeast Asia. The results were terror and poverty, mass deportations, a Vietnamese gulag and the horrors experienced by the boat people. And in Cambodia the result was one of the worst cases of genocide in twentieth-century history, the physical annihilation of anywhere between one fourth and one third of the Cambodian people by the Khmer Rouge regime. *This* is what our great humanitarian protest helped bring about.

In saying these things I'm not making a confession of guilt. As I said before, our intentions were morally unexceptionable, and one must make a careful distinction between guilt and responsibility. I believe that my major responsibility coming out of my (admittedly minor) part in this sad story is a firm resolve *never again* to be seduced into a politics of moral purity that disdains the calculus of means, costs and consequences. Of course we could not foresee the horrendous consequences cited just now, and I fervently hope that in a final judgment we will not be blamed for them. But the immediately relevant point is that *we did not try*. No one knows the future, but the responsible actor makes an effort to weigh possible futures and to gear his actions to this calculus.

Vietnam is more than an example. It has become the prototype of a politics of moral purity that has now been institutionalized in the United States and, to a lesser extent, in other Western democracies. The issues, of course, shift. Some are international, some domestic. What remains is a by now highly organized "constituency of conscience" (that arrogant self-designation also derives from the anti-war movement), centered in the elite cultural institutions and in the socially established churches, which habitually treats anyone who even asks a question about probable consequences as a moral pariah. And it is worth emphasizing that, of course, there are comparable communities of putative moral purity on the right of the American political spectrum. If this lecture were being delivered at, say, a Southern Baptist academy in Texas it would be important to develop this point; it would be pampering the audience to do so in Boston.

It would be useful to give one more example of what is at issue here, this one very recent indeed—the campaign for economic sanctions against South Africa. This is a situation that I have come to know rather well in the last two years and, let me say emphatically, I have no normative differences at all with anyone who judges that apartheid is a morally loathsome system.

But that is not the question here at all. Rather, the question is whether the particular economic measures advocated by the anti-apartheid movement (principally, disinvestment by American companies and various sanctions by the American government) are or are not likely to hasten the end of the present South African system. Let me also say that I don't know; nobody knows (and that includes eminent economists). Probably a lot depends on whether one thinks in a short-run or a long-run time frame. In the short run, it is now quite clear, Western economic measures directed against South Africa have led to consequences pretty much the opposite of those anticipated by the advocates: The South African economy is in a phase of modest recovery (partly fueled by the rise in the price of gold, which in turn, ironically, is due to nervousness about Western measures against South Africa). Far from being "brought to its knees," the South African government is more truculent than before, and it has gained greatly from anti-Western sentiments among white South Africans in the recent elections. In the same elections, the right wing has also gained, while the main anti-apartheid party participating in parliamentary politics has experienced a humiliating defeat. What should be most troubling to Americans is that the absence of quick results has led to a shift away from South Africa in public attention; there are now, it seems, more interesting matters to be morally outraged about. The costs of all of this, needless to say, are not borne by Americans but by black South Africans, who have been experiencing as yet moderate economic disloca- tions and a far from moderate increase in government repression.

This is not the appropriate occasion to discuss what Americans concerned for a non-racial democracy in South Africa can or cannot effectively do. My point here is simply that any action should first and foremost be concerned with results, with a careful calculus of consequences. It is no small thing to take actions that may cost human suffering and even human life in a faraway country. To do this without the most painstaking assessment of tradeoffs is morally irresponsible. To do it because it makes one feel morally pure is contemptible.

I have tried to show how a social-scientific perspective can be useful for a morally responsible politics that takes the empirical realities seriously. It is time now to approach a conclusion. I'm not quite sure how to conclude. Obviously not with some ringing inspirational message, since soberness, not enthusiasm, is the tone I have taken here. Perhaps it is appropriate to return once more to Max Weber.

When Weber used the word "vocation" (*Beruf*) to refer to politics he knew what associations he was invoking. He had, after all, discussed at great length the permutations of the Christian notion of vocation in his single most important book, *The Protestant Ethic and the Spirit of Capitalism*. A vocation is an occupation to which one is called—by God, by fate, by circumstance, perhaps by inner necessity. By implication some individuals may have this vocation, others not. I have never been persuaded by those (some on the left, some on the right) who have urged that everyone has the obligation to be politically active. It seems to me that this is a narrow, ultimately oppressive view of the political. Even in a democracy—perhaps especially in a democracy—one should concede the right of individuals *not* to be active in or even concerned with politics. Their vocation may be to care for the sick. Or to raise children. Or, for that matter, to paint ideograms on silk screens. But some of us *will* be called to political action, if not as a permanent occupation, then in certain situations or at certain junctures in our lives. This vocation has serious moral implications, some of which are closely related to the foregoing considerations.

It has been a commonplace of the so-called "policy sciences" (a self-contradictory category, I tend to think) that the more an actor knows about a situation, the more effective will he be in it. Probably so (though there is also something like an overload of information that can paralyze action, which has led one political scientist, Warren Ilchman, to coin the lovely phrase "optimal ignorance"). But the social scientist knows that however much we know about a situation, our knowledge will be incomplete and less than certain. Contrary to popular notions, science is the realm not of certainty, but of probabilities. The only certainties to be had in human life are in the realm of the *raison du coeur*; they are moral and religious, not scientific, in nature. Now, the scientist, whether in the human or the natural sciences, need not be bothered by this (unless science is the only meaning in his life—a rare and probably pathological condition). He can always say (and how many books in the social sciences end with such a statement!) that "more research is needed." Science, like art, is long. But life is short. The political actor cannot wait for the ever-receding conclusions of research. He is constrained to act now, and that means to act in a state of considerable ignorance. To act politically is to take risks. At times these risks are awesome.

The empirical risk, of course, is grounded in what, following Weber, could be called the "Iron Law of Unintended Consequences." We can, indeed (as I have just argued) we should, try to assess and foresee the consequences of our political actions. But any such assessment remains a probabilistic one. Ever again the consequences of our actions escape us and return to haunt us. The moral risk is that we will be responsible for the evil and the suffering that may be the costs of our actions. As the Apostle Paul put it in his letter to the Romans: "I can will what is right, but I cannot do it. For I do not do the good I want, but the evil I do not want is what I do." Paul did not have politics in mind, but the passage is singularly applicable to the sphere of political action. Put in secular terms, one cannot act politically without getting one's hands dirty. And sometimes, alas, one cannot act politically without getting blood on one's boots. This, if you will, is another Iron Law, that of *les mains sales*. Unless one deliberately closes one's eyes to this reality (I suppose that is the most common way of dealing with the matter), there are, I think, only two existential postures in which one can come to terms with it. The first is religious: Paul's understanding of justification by faith is a centrally important Christian version of this. The second is stoical—the fully aware shouldering of the burden of unintended evil that is part of the human condition. That, incidentally, was Max Weber's choice, an acceptance of tragedy bordering on the heroic. (Weber was once asked: "If this is what you think, why do you go on doing sociology?" He replied: "I want to see how much I can stand.") I have immense respect for this kind of stoicism, but, as some of you know, my own response to this existential dilemma is religious; indeed it is, *stricto sensu*, Pauline.

The social sciences, to repeat, teach us a particular version of the "art of mistrust." By the same token, they are intrinsically anti-utopian. Especially sociology has, from its beginnings, been marked by a debunking spirit—looking beneath and behind the facades of social life, dragging dirty secrets out into the open (as, for instance, all the dirty secrets of class), unmasking the vested interests lurking behind lofty rhetoric—if you will, a certifiably subversive enterprise. It is ironic that so many sociologists, inveterate skeptics when it comes to the present, have been mistily credulous about the future. It seems to me that sociological skepticism must apply not only to the status quo but to any political agenda purporting to replace the status quo. This applies with particular urgency to the two great utopian fantasies of the modern era, the myth of progress and the myth of revolution.

I have repeatedly used words that some of you, especially if you are still young, may find chilling—"caution," "soberness," "carefulness." Are these not words that portend paralysis? With all this skepticism and all this cautiousness, will one not inevitably end up doing nothing at all? And, in consequence, abandon the political arena to the crooks and the fanatics who have no such fine scruples? My answer, emphatically and passionately, is *No! By no means!* I think that one can show that careless actions have done much greater harm in history than inaction caused by carefulness. But, be this as it may, there is no reason why caution should lead to inaction. If that were true, none of us would ever trust ourselves into the hands of a surgeon. I believe that the vocation of political action requires no less responsibility than that of surgery. And in both vocations a core norm should be that portion of the Hippocratic oath that enjoins the physician above all not to do greater harm.

9

Religious Liberty— Sub Specie Ludi*

To be expected to listen to an after-dinner presentation at the conclusion of a conference as heavy as this one may not be an infringement of religious liberty, but could easily be construed as a violation of *some* fundamental human right. Any jurist faithful to the doctrine of original intent will surely agree that this expectation violates the constitutional proscription of cruel and unusual punishment. However, having been cleverly seduced into inflicting this punishment on you, I suppose that at this late date, I'll have to go through with it. There is one thing I can do in mitigation, and that is to be brief. It is for this reason that I decided to put my observations into a written text, since, like most aging professors, I'm likely to go on for the full length of a three-hour seminar if I speak from notes (at which point even the most liberal among you might reassess your position on the venerable Southern institution of tarring and feathering).

My assignment is to speak about religious liberty in

*Williamsburg Charter conference, 1988

167

a global context, making sure to touch upon its relationship to the totalitarian state and to the growth of fundamentalist movements, and to do so in a light, entertaining manner. This reminds me of the story of the man who tried to interest a publisher in a book titled *How I Hunted Bears in the Woods of Maine*. After being advised by the marketing people that the book should not offend environmentalists, should have some sexual interest, and should be both timely and inspiring, the author succeeded in getting the book accepted under the revised title *How I Made Love to a Bear in the Woods of Maine, Under Orders from Ollie North, and Found God*.

Trying not to bore you, I may already be succeeding in offending you. Am I not approaching a very serious subject in a reprehensibly frivolous manner? Well, let me respond to this charge by stating the single thesis I want to put to you this evening: *The hidden purpose of religious liberty is to protect the possibility of laughter in this world*.

In recent discussions of the place of religious liberty in the American polity a number of people have argued that religious liberty is the first liberty, that it is the foundation, the *fons et origo*, of all the other rights and liberties. I'm not sure that I agree with this or am competent to evaluate all these arguments, but I agree with the basic proposition, and I do so for one, overridingly important reason: The polity that recognizes religious liberty as a fundamental human right *ipso facto* recognizes (knowingly or unknowingly) the limits of political power. At the core of man's religious quest is the experience of transcendence, the encounter with a reality that is "totally other" than all the realities of ordinary life. And a necessary consequence of this encounter is that all the ordinary realities, including the most imposing and oppressive ones, are relativized. In the realm of human institutions, none is more imposing and (at least potentially) more oppressive than the polity, especially in its recent embodiment as the modern state, which is a historically unprecedented agglomeration of power. This characteristic, of course, is manifested most terrifyingly in the modern totalitarian state, but all contemporary states, even the most democratic ones, possess instruments of power that would have made the most awesome tyrants of antiquity green with envy. (Think of what Genghis Khan could have done with radio communications, or the Emperor Caligula with an internal revenue service!) The state is very serious business indeed, *deadly* business (for in the end every state, even the most peaceful one, rests on the power of the sword), and those who represent the state take themselves very seriously. That is why the state always wraps itself in religious or quasi-religious symbols, why it fosters solemn ceremonies, and why the refusal to be serious about the state is everywhere a punishable offense (from *lèse-majesté* to contempt of Congress). Given all this, it should not surprise us that there is a built-in tension between all institutions of political power and the religious quest that tends toward relativizing them.

This has always been so. The holders of political power have always tried to contain the potentially subversive force of religion by controlling religious institutions. Most of the time they have been successful in this, but ever again there appeared religious spokesmen—emissaries of transcendence, if you will—who refused to play the roles of legitimators of the political status quo. The power-holders naturally took a very dim view of these troublemakers and frequently enough they employed very disagreeable methods to deal with the trouble. The more tyrannical the ruler, the more urgent was the need to shut up the troublemakers. In the biblical tradition, of course, the figure of the prophet most clearly represents this religious challenge to the self-important seriousness of the rulers of this world—prototypically, in the confrontation between Nathan and King David. This drama of speaking transcendent truth to worldly power has been re-enacted many times in the history of Judaism, Christianity and Islam, the three great streams flowing out of the biblical experience. It should be stressed, though, that comparable relativizations of the polity have occurred in other traditions. The figures of Antigone and Socrates embody it in classical antiquity, as do a long line of Hindu sages, Buddhist monks and Confucian scholars. All human religions are windows on the vastness of the transcendent: Open any one of these windows, and the glitter of political power suddenly reveals itself to be a rather shabby affair.

It is precisely in this quality of relativizing, unmasking, debunking the pretensions of human power that we can see the deep affinity between the religious and the comic, between the prophet and the clown.

The prophet proclaims that God laughs at all the kings and emperors of the earth; the clown makes a joke and reveals that the emperor has no clothes. Tyrants are afraid of prophecy and of jokes. The tyrants of modern totalitarianism, very logically, have been as assiduous in controlling the institutions that (heaven forbid) may bring forth prophets as they have been in persecuting anyone who dared to make jokes about their grimly serious agendas. And this is why churches have become the last refuge of dissenters in all totalitarian societies, and why the same societies have produced a luxurious growth of underground humor.

Eastern Europe, I suppose, has been the most fertile ground for this kind of relativizing (and, in the deepest sense of the word, redeeming) humor. It is the year 2088. Two Czechs are standing on Wenceslas Square in Prague, in front of the Lumumba Monument. There is a long silence, and then one says to the other: "You know, it was better under the Chinese." There was the man who walked into a state department store in Leipzig and asked for undershirts. The salesperson told him: "You have to go to the third floor. There they have no undershirts. On this floor we have no shirts." Some of you, I expect, know the Soviet stories about the mythical radio station in Erivan to which listeners may send questions. Question to Radio Erivan: "Is it not true that the Soviet government governs much better than did the Tsarist government?'' Radio Erivan answers: ''Yes, of course.'' Question: ''Yet it seems that the Tsarist government was more popular. Why is that?'' Answer: ''Because it governed *less*.'' When people laugh at such jokes in Prague or in Leningrad it is as if, for one joyful moment, the prison walls of the totalitarian society are breached, transcended (precisely), and a window opens up on the fresh air of freedom. And, whatever the differences between these experiences, this is just what happens as people gather in barely tolerated churches and synagogues to worship a God who is more powerful than all the tyrants of this world.

A believing Jew or Christian can put this insight into a theological proposition: Redemption will finally be experienced as comic relief on a cosmic scale, and even now, in an as-yet-unredeemed world, redemption can be anticipated as a healing joke. Let me assure you that if I had the time, I would be prepared to defend this proposition with as much seriousness as anyone could desire, indeed with the *utmost* seriousness (the ultimate joke is of the very essence of seriousness; only penultimate jokes are frivolous). But this, truly, cannot be done after dinner at the tail end of a conference. Let me add this, though: If I were to theologize about this, I would do it as a believing Christian. But I'm certain that my view about the primacy of religious liberty in a catalogue of liberties would remain the same if tomorrow I should lose my faith and should redefine myself as an agnostic (an unlikely contingency, I'm happy to say, but not one beyond an exercise of the imagination). As an agnostic I would also be concerned that human existence not be confined in the prison of ordinary reality, and even if I would now be unable to make positive affirmations about the nature of that which transcends our ordinary lives, I would not want steel bars to be imposed on every window that might, conceivably, open up on unthought-of possibilities. In other words, there is a *secular* argument to be made for the primacy of religious liberty, as there are secular reasons for the democratic option against the totalitarian temptations of our age.

This brings me to a paradox, which is particularly relevant to current debates over the meaning of the first amendment in the United States. I can claim no expertise in the constitutional and juridical ramifications of this issue. But it seems to me that there is a depressing triviality about much that has been said about "secular purpose" in this or that activity of religious institutions, including some things that have been said about this by the Supreme Court. Let me not dwell here on the remarkable spectacle of these nine characters, who swish around in priestly robes in a building resembling a Greek temple and engage in the endless exegesis of a sacred text and then have the *chutzpah* to insist that there is no establishment of religion in America. To be sure, there is a "secular purpose" served if a church runs a soup kitchen, an orphanage or even (though this is more doubtful) a university. But the most important "secular purpose" any church can serve is to remind people that there is a meaning to human existence that transcends all worldly agendas, that all human institutions (including the nation-state) are only relatively important and are ultimately not to be taken seriously, and that all worldly authority (even that of the Supreme Court of the United States) is disclosed to be comically irrelevant in the perspective of transcendence. This, then, is the paradox: Religious institutions serve their most important secular purpose precisely when they are *least secular* in their activities. Society, under certain circumstances, can easily dispense with church-operated soup kitchens or universities. Society can ill afford to lose the reminders of transcendence that the church provides every time it worships God. The protection of religious liberty serves the purpose of this ultimate anamnesis, which *ipso facto* protects the possibility of laughter and the wondrous mystery of the human condition.

I do not share the view that democracy is the noblest form of government, even less the Wilsonian messianism that would see the United States as the providential instrument by which democracy is to be imposed on every nation on earth (a messianism, incidentally, to which the American right is as prone as the American left—the two only differ as to *which* recalcitrant countries are to be the objects of the democratic crusade). Rather, I'm inclined to agree with Winston Churchill that democracy is an appalling business—until one considers the alternatives, or at least those that are available under modern conditions. The modern state, for reasons rooted in its very structure, contains the impulse to expand into every nook and cranny of society. The totalitarian state is, of course, the apotheosis (I choose the word deliberately) of this impulse. Democracy provides the only halfway reliable institutional mechanisms to curb the totalitarian impulse. It doesn't do this because of its ideology. There have been cases of what J. L. Talmon called "totalitarian democracy," at least in the sphere of ideas (Jacobinism in its original version); sometimes, alas, in the sphere of facts. But the core of Western democracy, and certainly of the democratic experiment of the United States, is the institutionalization of limits on the power of government. Political scientists have defined democracy in different ways; most come down to two key elements—regular elections and some sort of bill of rights. In other words, democracy seeks to ensure (not sporadically, but through predictable institutions" that the rascals can be thrown out from time to time and that there are certain things that they can't do while they're in. Democracy (not as an idea, but as a functioning political reality) is based on suspicion and irreverence—which is precisely why it is the best shield against the totalitarian project, which demands faith and veneration. Any democratic constitution must say to the state, repetitively and insistently: "Thus far, and no farther!" Every protection of political liberties and of human rights, of course, does just that. The recognition of religious liberty, as a fundamental and irrevocable right, does it in a fundamental way. Religious liberty is not one of many benefits that the state may choose to bestow on its subjects; rather, religious liberty is rooted in the very nature of man and, when the state recognizes it, the state *ipso facto* bows before a sovereignty that radically transcends every worldly manifestation of power. For the religious believer, of course, this is the sovereignty of God; for the agnostic it will be the sovereignty of that mystery within man that ever thrives to go beyond the given—the mystery of man's freedom.

It seems to me that these considerations have very practical implications for many of the controversies currently dividing American society. We have reason to be grateful that this society is democratically governed, that controversy is possible and indeed protected, and that by and large religious liberty is secure. However, it would be very foolish to overlook the totalitarian tendencies even within this society, some of them very much present in issues touching on religious liberty. I do not have the time to spell this out; suffice it to say that one of the hallmarks of the totalitarian project is always the urge to drive underground the metaphysical propensity in man, to banish transcendence from the public square (except in the domesticated form of established or civil religion), and to make all of social life subject to the trivial worldview of functional rationality. Put simply, the totalitarian project requires a world without windows; the defense of religious liberty is the counter-project of keeping open the windows on the wonder of our condition.

How well have I carried out my assignment thus far? Well, I've certainly said some things about religious liberty and about totalitarianism, I've been reasonably global, and I've made some feeble attempts at being entertaining. What have I left out? Ah, yes—there is still the little matter of fundamentalism. Let me try. The problem, of course, is that one man's fundamentalism is another's self-evident truth. Depending on where you happen to live, the word may evoke Communist party officials trying to preserve Marxist-Leninist orthodoxy, ayatollahs putting women behind veils, or born-again seminary trustees firing professors for not teaching that Moses wrote the Pentateuch. I happen to live two blocks from the Charles River; when *I* hear the word "fundamentalism," I think of my academic colleagues and neighbors whose unbending convictions and self-righteous intolerance of heretics are fully up to ayatollah standards (though, thank God, they lack ayatollah means of enforcement). Perhaps we can be satisfied here with an *ad hoc* definition of fundamentalism as any all-embracing system of belief held with rigid certitude and coupled with the moral assurance of one's right to impose it on everyone else. Fundamentalism thus understood, whatever its ideational content, will always be an enemy of religious liberty; always and everywhere, it can only flourish behind tightly shut windows; and wherever it sees an open window, it is under the urgent compulsion to slam it shut.

It is undoubtedly correct to say that through most of human history most fanaticism has been religious. This is a source of sorrow for any religious believer. It is a source of sorrow for me as a Christian who believes that not only is it possible to be religious without being fanatical, genuine religious faith *precludes* fanaticism. In the contemporary world too, sad to say, there has been a notable upsurge of religious fundamentalisms. The most dramatic cases of this, of course, are Islamic and Protestant fundamentalism, both enormously powerful forces crossnationally and both (though there are very important differences between them) capable of inspiring large numbers of people to make radical changes in their lives. Other religious traditions, however, have shown themselves capable of quite similar outbursts of unlovely and, at times, homicidal fanaticism. Let me just mention both Catholics and Protestants in Northern Ireland, every sect of Islam and Christianity in Lebanon, Jewish fundamentalists in Israel, both Hindus and Buddhists in Sri Lanka,

Sikhs in the Punjab, and an odd assortment of syncretistic cults all across sub-Saharan Africa. Let me say that I'm unpersuaded by those who regard Protestant fundamentalism in this country as constituting a comparable danger to pluralism and to civic peace, but let it be stipulated that there are situations in America too where religious liberty is threatened by religious fanaticism (I would certainly think so if I were a seminary professor about to be fired for teaching modern methods of biblical scholarship, though, even in my distress, I would console myself with the knowledge that my persecutors cannot call upon the police to assist them).

All the same, speaking in America to what I assume is a largely college-educated audience, I must say that the most pervasive fundamentalisms facing us here are secular ones. Politically, they are both of the left and the right; in the milieu of the new knowledge class in America, it would be indulging the audience to go on about the right (as when, in an act he himself, modestly, described as one of courage, the former president of Yale University denounced the Moral Majority). In this milieu there is bemused contempt about the "superstitions" of religious fundamentalists, such as their belief that the Bible is literally inspired or that prayer can cause miracles. As a theologically liberal Lutheran, I must confess that I find the first proposition improbable and that I'm inclined to skepticism about any concrete specification of the second. But among the cultured despisers of Jerry Falwell and his cohorts it is widely believed that the Soviet Union has changed fundamentally because it has the first leader with clothes that fit, that the establishment of racial quotas is a means toward a race-blind society, or that a six-month fetus should have a legal status roughly comparable to a wart. It seems to me that here we have "superstitions" greatly more dangerous than those found in the Protestant hinterland. It is the values and prejudices of the knowledge class, *not* those of the Reverend Falwell, that today shape important policies, are enacted into law and define what is culturally acceptable. It is primarily against *them*, and not against the subculture of conservative Protestantism, that religious liberty must be protected. It is precisely the knowledge class which today seeks an "establishment of religion"—that is, the imposition through state power of its particular worldview and morality—and which interferes with the "free exercise of religion" of those who disagree with its ideology.

The social psychology of all fundamentalisms, religious or secular, holds no great enigmas. Its core motive is what Erich Fromm called the "escape from freedom"—the flight into an illusionary and necessarily intolerant certitude from the insecurities of being human. In all likelihood this motive is age-old, but it takes on a special force under the circumstances of modernity. I have written extensively on this matter and I cannot possibly develop fully my understanding of it here; I can only assert that there is a dialectical relation between the multiplication of choices brought about by modern pluralism and the flight into a once-and-for-all choice posited as an absolute. The affirmation of religious liberty by contrast repudiates such illusory absolutes. It may take a believing or a skeptical form. The latter will be a stoic acceptance of uncertainty; the former is based on the recognition that faith does not require false certitudes, that it can even live with doubt. This is why the fanatic cannot laugh (an incapacity he shares with the totalitarian). Faith, on the other hand, opens up the possibility of laughter at the most profound level—the laughter that participates, in anticipation, in the joyful play of the angels.

Some of you may have heard the story of the young rabbi who left Eastern Europe sometime around the turn of the century to serve a congregation in America. When he went to say goodbye to his teacher, the latter said to him: "God bless you, my son. And always remember: Life is like a cup of tea." Often, in the years that followed, the rabbi wondered what the old man had meant by this cryptic remark. Then, after many years, he had occasion to make a return visit to his hometown. The old man was still alive and, while visiting him, the rabbi decided to ask him. "You will remember," he said, "that when I left for America and you gave me your blessing, you said that I should always remember that life is like a cup of tea. I've often wondered what you meant. Please tell me now: What *did* you mean?" The old man shook his head and asked; "Is that what I said to you?" "Yes, that's what you said. What does it mean?" There was a long silence. Then the old man said: "*Nu*, maybe life is *not* like a cup of tea."

10 Concluding Remarks—A Rumor of Angels

"Everything is full of gods," exclaimed Thales of Miletus. Biblical monotheism swept away the gods in the glorification of the awesome majesty of the One, but the fullness that overwhelmed Thales continued to live on for a long time in the figures of the angels, those beings of light who are witness to the fullness of the divine glory. In the prophetic visions they surround the throne of God. Again and again, in the pages of both the Old and New Testaments, they appear as messengers (*angeloi*) of this God, signalizing His transcendence as well as His presence in the world of man. Above all, angels signal God's concern for this world, both in judgment and in redemption. Nothing is left out of this concern. As a rabbinical writer put it, "There's not a stalk on earth that has not its (protecting or guardian) angel in heaven."[50] In the religious view of reality, all phenomena point toward that which transcends them, and this transcendence actively impinges from all sides on the empirical sphere of human existence.

179

It was only with the onset of secularization that the divine fullness began to recede, until the point was reached when the empirical sphere became both all-encompassing and perfectly closed in upon itself. At that point man was truly alone in reality. We have come a long way from the gods and from the angels. The breaches of this-worldly reality which these mighty figures embodied have increasingly vanished from our consciousness as serious possibilities. They linger on as fairy tales, nostalgias, perhaps as vague symbols of some sort. A few years ago, a priest working in a slum section of a European city was asked why he was doing it, and replied, "So that the rumor of God may not disappear completely." The word aptly expresses what the signals of transcendence have become in our situation—rumors—and not very reputable rumors at that.

This book has not been about angels. At best, it might be a preface to angelology, if by that one meant a study of God's messengers as His signals in reality. We are, whether we like it or not, in a situation in which transcendence has been reduced to a rumor. We cannot escape our situation with one magical jump. We cannot readily, and probably should not wish to, return to an earlier situation in the history of man's grappling with reality. For this reason I have taken pains, at a number of points in my argument, to stress that what I am advocating is neither esoteric nor "reactionary." But I have also tried to show that our situation is not an inexorable fate and that secularized consciousness is not the absolute it presents itself as. We must begin in the situation in which we find ourselves, but we must not submit to it as to an irresistible tyranny. If the signals of transcendence have become rumors in our time, then we can set out to explore these rumors—and perhaps to follow them up to their source.

A rediscovery of the supernatural will be, above all, a regaining of openness in our perception of reality. It will not only be, as theologians influenced by existentialism have greatly overemphasized, an overcoming of tragedy. Perhaps more importantly it will be an overcoming of triviality. In openness to the signals of transcendence the true proportions of our experience are rediscovered. This is the comic relief of redemption; it makes it possible for us to laugh and to play with a new fullness. This in no way implies a remoteness from the moral challenges of the moment, but rather the most careful attention to each human gesture that we encounter or that we may be called upon to perform in the everyday dramas of human life—literally, an "infinite care" in the affairs of men—just because, in the words of the New Testament writer, it is in the midst of these affairs that "some have entertained angels unawares." (Hebrews 13:2)

I think that the openness and the reproportioning this attitude entails have a moral significance, even a political significance, of no mean degree. The principal moral benefit of religion is that it permits a confrontation with the age in which one lives in a perspective that transcends the age and thus puts it in proportion. This both vindicates courage and safeguards against fanaticism. To find courage to do what must be done in a given moment is not the only moral good. It is also very much a moral good that this same moment does not become the be-all and end-all of one's existence, that in meeting its demands one does not lose the capacity to laugh and to play. One must have experienced the grim humorlessness of contemporary revolutionary ideologies to appreciate fully the humanizing power of the religious perspective. It is hardly necessary to insist here on the moral demands of our situation, especially in America today; they stagger the imagination. Whether we approach them in a mood of doomsday or of renewed hope in the efficacy of particular programs of action often depends on whether we have just read the morning or the afternoon paper. In either case one of the best things that can happen to us is to recall that, to use Dietrich Bonhoeffer's suggestive term, all historical events are "penultimate," that their ultimate significance lies in a reality that transcends them and that transcends all the empirical coordinates of human existence.

For most of this book I have discussed the rediscovery of the supernatural as a possibility for theological thought in our time. It is impossible to know for sure whether any such rediscovery will remain the property of more or less isolated cognitive minorities, or whether it may also have an impact of larger historical dimensions. It is possible to speculate, even to venture prognoses, on the basis of what is empirically knowable in the present, but all "futurology" is a tenuous business. The sociologist and probably any other empirical observer of human events will be tempted to prognosticate, and I too have yielded to the temptation earlier. But I would like to emphasize once more that anyone who approaches religion with an interest in its possible truth, rather than in this or that aspect of its social manifestations, would do well to cultivate a measure of indifference in the matter of empirical prognoses. History brings out certain questions of truth, makes certain answers more or less accessible, constructs and disintegrates plausibility structures. But the historical course of the question about transcendence cannot, of itself, answer the question. It is only human to be exhilarated if one thinks one is riding on the crest of the future. All too often, however, such exhilaration gives way to the sobering recognition that what looked like a mighty wave of history was only a marginal eddy in the stream of events. For the theologian, if not for the social scientist, I would therefore suggest a moratorium on the anxious query as to just who it is that has modernity by the short hair. Theology must begin and end with the question of truth. My concern here has been with some possible methods of pursuing this question today.

Notes

1. Thomas J. J. Altizer and William Hamilton, *Radical Theology and the Death of God* (Indianapolis, Bobbs-Merrill, 1966), p. 11.
2. Herman Kahn and Anthony J. Wiener, *The Year 2000—A Framework for Speculation on the Next Thirty-three Years* (New York, Macmillan, 1967), p. 7 (Table I).
3. Alfred Schutz, *Collected Papers* (The Hague, Nijhoff, 1962), vol. I, p. 208.
4. Thomas Luckmann, *The Invisible Religion—The Problem of Religion in Modern Society* (New York, Macmillan, 1967).
5. Most of these studies are not available in English. However, cf. the English-language journal of this group, *Social Compass*, published in Europe, as well as the American Catholic Council journal *Sociological Analysis*. Also, cf. the very useful reference work edited by Hervé Carrier and Emile Pin, *Sociology of Christianity—An International Bibliography* (Rome, Gregorian University Press, 1964). For the flavor of this approach, cf. the contributions of F. Boulard, F.-A. Isambert and Emile Pin in the reader edited by Louis Schneider, *Religion, Culture and Society* (New York, Wiley, 1964), pp. 385ff., 400ff., and 411ff.
6. Cf. Charles Glock and Rodney Stark, *Religion and Society in Tension* (Chicago, Rand McNally, 1965); N. J. Demerath II, *Social Class in American Protestantism* (Chicago, Rand McNally, 1965); Charles Glock, Benjamin Ringer and Earl Babbie, *To Com-*

183

fort and to Challenge—A Dilemma of the Contemporary Church (Berkeley, University of California Press, 1967). The most important recent sociological study of American religion is still Gerhard Lenski, *The Religious Factor* (Garden City, N.Y., Doubleday, 1961).

7. For a systematic presentation of this, in terms of the sociology of knowledge, cf. Peter Berger and Thomas Luckmann, *The Social Construction of Reality* (Garden City, N.Y., Doubleday, 1966).

8. Cf. ibid., pp. 135ff. On the social-psychological processes involved in this, cf. Solomon Asch, *Social Psychology* (New York, Prentice-Hall, 1952), pp. 387ff.

9. Walter Kaufmann, *Nietzsche* (New York, Meridian Books, 1956), p. 81.

10. Cf. my "A Sociological View of the Secularization of Theology," *Journal for the Scientific Study of Religion*, Spring 1967, for a more detailed analysis of this constellation.

11. In a recent (unpublished) radio talk, "Sociologist Fallen Among Secular Theologians."

12. For a discussion of the religious dilemma of contemporary Judaism, cf. Arthur Cohen, *The Natural and the Supernatural Jew—A History and Theological Introduction* (New York, Pantheon Books, 1962).

13. Cf. Peter Berger and Thomas Luckmann, "Secularization and Pluralism," *International Yearbook for the Sociology of Religion*, 1966.

14. Cf. my *The Sacred Canopy—Elements of a Sociological Theory of Religion* (Garden City, N.Y., Doubleday, 1967), pp. 105ff.

15. On the contemporary religious market, cf. Berger and Luckmann, "Secularization and Pluralism," loc. cit.

16. Cf. Louis Pauwels and Jacques Bergier, *The Morning of the Magicians* (New York, Stein and Day, 1964).

17. Rose Goldsen et al., *What College Students Think* (Princeton, N.J., Nostrand, 1960).

18. Poll conducted on behalf of the news magazine *Der Spiegel* (21:52, December 18, 1967).

19. David Martin, *A Sociology of English Religion* (New York, Basic Books, 1967), p. 75.

20. Cf. John Petrie (ed.), *The Worker Priests—A Collective Documentation* (London, Routledge and Kegan Paul, 1956).

21. Cf. Ernest Campbell and Thomas Pettigrew, *Christians in Racial Crisis—A Study of Little Rock's Ministry* (Washington, Public Affairs Press, 1959).

22. Cf. Berger and Luckmann, *Social Construction of Reality*, especially pp. 85ff., and my *Sacred Canopy*, especially pp. 126ff.

23. I made this distinction myself in an earlier discussion of some of these questions, *The Precarious Vision* (Garden City, N.Y., Doubleday, 1961); I must now disavow this approach.

24. Ludwig Feuerbach, *The Essence of Christianity* (New York, Harper, 1957), pp. xff.

25. Again, cf. Berger and Luckmann, "Secularization and Pluralism," loc. cit. Some of the social-psychological aspects of this interpretation of pluralism are derived from the work of the contemporary German sociologists Arnold Gehlen and Helmut Schelsky.

26. For a systematic development of this, again cf. my *Sacred Canopy*.

27. There is, of course, a vast literature on these theological developments, but one of the most useful analyses in English is still H. R. Mackintosh, *Types of Modern Theology*. Of the standard works in German, I have found Horst Stephan and Martin Schmidt, *Geschichte der deutschen evangelischen Theologie* very useful.

28. Albert Camus, *The Plague* (New York, Knopf, 1948), p. 278.

29. Again cf. my *Sacred Canopy*, especially cc. 1–2.

30. Eric Voegelin, *Order and History* (Baton Rouge, Louisiana State University Press, 1956), vol. I ("Israel and Revelation"), p. ix.

31. Cf. Johan Huizinga, *Homo Ludens—A Study of the Play Element in Culture* (Boston, Beacon Press, 1955).

32. On this cf. Schutz, op. cit.

33. *"Alle Lust will Ewigkeit—will tiefe, tiefe Ewigkeit!"*—Friedrich Nietzsche, *Also sprach Zarathustra* (Leipzig, Kroener, 1917), p. 333.

34. C. S. Lewis, *The Weight of Glory* (Grand Rapids, Mich., Eerdmans, 1965), pp. 44f.

35. Among Catholics by Karl Rahner, among Protestants by Jürgen Moltmann and Wolfhart Pannenberg.

36. These theological developments are very important, not only because of the specific attention they give to the phenomenon of hope, but because they take seriously the possibility of an anthropological starting point for theology. It seems to me, however, that the emphasis on hope as *the* theologically relevant anthropological element is far too narrow. This can probably be accounted for by two circumstances—among Protestants, the interest in affirming, against neo-orthodoxy, the empirical historicity of the Christian religion (which is then related to hope as an essential mode of the "futurity" of man)—among both Protestants and Catholics, the elaboration of these ideas in the dialogue with Marxism (in which Christian hope is set off against Marxist eschatology). I share the animus against the neo-orthodox treatment of empirical history as well as the concern for a dialogue with Marxism, but would still insist on a much broader anthropological focus.

37. Philip Rieff, *Freud—The Mind of the Moralist* (Garden City, N.Y., Doubleday-Anchor, 1961), pp. 329ff.

38. An earlier version of this argument may be found in my *Precarious Vision*, pp. 209ff. I have not changed my mind about this and what I say here is substantially a repetition.

39. Sigmund Freud, "Wit and Its Relation to the Unconscious," in A. A. Brill (ed.), *The Basic Writings of Sigmund Freud* (New York, Modern Library, 1938): Henri Bergson, "Laughter," in W. Sypher (ed.), *Comedy* (Garden City, N.Y., Doubleday-Anchor, 1956).

40. Bergson, op. cit., p. 123.

41. Alfred Schutz, "Don Quixote and the Problem of Reality," in *Collected Papers* (The Hague, Nijhoff, 1964), vol. II, p. 157.

42. Enid Welsford, *The Fool* (Garden City, N.Y., Doubleday-Anchor, 1961), pp. 326ff.

43. This idea is developed systematically in *Sacred Canopy*, cc. 1–2.

44. Cf. Geoffrey Gorer, *Death, Grief and Mourning* (Garden City, N.Y., Doubleday, 1965). A good summation of the sociological import of this is a recent article by Philippe Ariès, *European Journal of Sociology*, 1967:2. Also cf. Barney Glaser and Anselm

Strauss, *Awareness of Dying* (Chicago, Aldine, 1965), for an empirical study of this in a hospital setting.

45. *De praedestinatione sanctorum*, 2:5.

46. Wolfhart Pannenberg et al., *Offenbarung als Geschichte* (Göttingen, Vandenhöck & Ruprecht, 1963). The work has recently come out in an English version.

47. As far as I understand him, Pannenberg seems to be in accord with this idea. My remarks here are not intended as criticism of Pannenberg, but rather as a *caveat* against the premature "correlations" to which theologians with a biographical and existential standpoint within a particular tradition are understandably prone.

48. Paul Tillich, *The Protestant Era* (Chicago, University of Chicago Press, 1948), p. 163.

49. The following remarks, of course, contain allusions to a variety of theological positions and controversies. The theologically informed reader will readily identify these (and, more likely than not, deplore their application!). I have felt, though, that nothing would be gained by studding these paragraphs with references, which would only detract from consideration of the possibilities or impossibility of such an approach.

50. Cited in Gustav Davidson, *A Dictionary of Angels* (New York, Free Press, 1967), p. xv.